INFORMATION ILLUSTRATION

Dale Glasgow

With Dan Elasky

Learn how to create imaginative diagrams,
charts, maps, and symbols
on the computer

Addison-Wesley Publishing Company

Reading, Massachusetts • Menlo Park, California • New York
Don Mills, Ontario • Wokingham, England • Amsterdam
Bonn • Sydney • Singapore • Tokyo • Madrid • San Juan
Paris • Seoul • Milan • Mexico City • Taipei

The illustrations in this book were created with the following software programs: Adobe Dimensions 1.0; Adobe Illustrator 5.0; Adobe Photoshop 2.5; Aldus FreeHand 4.0; Specular International Infini-D 2.5.2.

Many of the designations used by manufacturers and sellers to distinguish their products are claimed as trademarks. Where those designations appear in this book, and the publisher was aware of a trademark claim, the designations have been printed in initial capital letters or all capital letters.

The authors and publishers have taken care in preparation of this book, but make no expressed or implied warranty of any kind and assume no responsibility for errors or omissions. No liability is assumed for incidental or consequential damages in connection with or arising out of the use of the information or programs contained herein.

Library of Congress Cataloging-in-Publication Data has been applied for.

ISBN 0-201-40725-6

Cover design by Dale Glasgow
Text design by Dashton Parham

Set in Berkeley Oldstyle ITC by BT, 8 point.

Imagesetting by Advance Laser Graphics, Washington, D.C.

Manufactured in Hong Kong by Everbest Printing Company.

First printing, 1994

Addison-Wesley books are available for bulk purchases by corporations, institutions, and other organizations. For more information about how to make such purchases in the United States, please contact the Corporate, Government, and Special Sales Department at 1-800-238-9682.

ACKNOWLEDGEMENTS

I would like to thank

My family: Sharon, my wife and best friend, who has patiently allowed us to have our own business; Heather, Jennifer, Hannah, and Rachel, who break up the long days with the joy of innocence.

Dan, who, through the pain of telling how I work, never lost sight of the end.

Dash, who made visual sense out of the thousands of pictures.

My Mom and Dad, who thought I might do something with drawing cars and trucks.

My God Jesus, who has never failed me when I needed one more job to pay for the food on the table.

TABLE OF CONTENTS

INTRODUCTION

I nformation illustration has been practiced as a serious discipline for a long, long time. In North America it perhaps originated with the cave-dwelling clan leader who made the first technical diagram, showing the proper way to corner a sabre-toothed cat. The cat, painted on the cave wall, is simplified and stylized, as are the hunters and their weapons.

Or maybe it was the first chartist. She painted and regularly updated the first bar chart, with the bars showing "number of buffalo killed, by brave." She devised a template so she wouldn't have to re-invent the wheel every time she put a new brave into the data base. The chart bars were represented by a chief's headdress feathers. Or perhaps by a column of buffalo skulls.

But no, the first information illustrator was probably a map maker.

What a thrill it must have been for him, having compiled, synthesized, and rendered with crude pigments on a wall his notes and sketches of landforms and landmarks—and intuiting, perhaps, some unit of measurement which would wait for Egyptians or Phoenicians to lay down formally.

He's thinking, smugly, "I have here, right on my wall, a total grasp of this expanse of land." (I'd love to know what the first map was *of*.)

MODERN TIMES

From those not-so-humble beginnings to around 1986, things stayed pretty much the same in the world of information illustration: it always took a goodly amount of time to create an info-graphic.

Whether the illustrator used primitive pigments, pen and ink, or an airbrush, it must have always been frustratingly slow. It was in most cases impossible to change your mind halfway through and make major revisions; you had to start over.

Even if you had a clear conception of your image at the outset and carried it straight through to the end, there were always tasks which were extremely tedious: constructing irregular objects; making complex curves; rendering continuous tones; drawing perspective lines; and rendering and distorting repetitive shapes.

ELECTRONIC ILLUSTRATION

Then, in 1986 and 1987, powerful illustration and painting software started to become available for the Macintosh and other graphically oriented microcomputers; and suddenly it was possible to be an electronic illustrator. Almost every type of rendering and effect that you could do with traditional drawing tools could now be done, in far less time, on the computer screen.

These software programs have been steadily improved in the years since, and they now have such power, finesse, and speed that it's difficult for most of us to consider going back to pens and templates and airbrushes.

The decision to become a computer-based illustrator, however, is a major one. You must spend hundreds of hours researching, comparing, and testing all sorts of hardware and software. Then you have to fork out many thousands of dollars to buy the stuff. Then all you have to do is learn how to use it.

And, unfortunately, the process never ends. If you're like me, you'll keep on researching, evaluating, buying, and learning. Electronic illustration is an exciting profession; it's also extremely demanding. It can be financially rewarding; it certainly is financially draining. It can be maddening and frustrating; but it can also be extremely satisfying and, most of the time, it's fun.

I've written this book to introduce you to computer-based information illustration, and to help you decide to seriously consider it as a career.

I'm not comfortable with trying to say exactly what an information illustration is; I'd rather try to say what it is we do, most of the time. We take a set of facts, numbers, categories, structural parts, spatial relationships, or other information, simplify it without distorting it, and present it in an instantly graspable and visually engaging way.

Conversely, I think information illustrations are not *primarily* concerned with setting moods, motivating people, propagandizing overtly, commenting ironically, arousing emotions, selling goods, or making jokes—although an illustration or its accompanying text may do some of these things. The aim of an information illustration is to *inform:* to show or symbolize things as they *are,* not as someone thinks they should be.

THE PLAN OF THE BOOK

I begin with a "Gallery" chapter, in which I show you a variety of differ

ent illustrations I've done on the Macintosh since 1987.

In Chapter 2, we look at the layout of my electronic studio, and discuss the various hardware and software components of my system. I try to give you a lot of recommendations and advice on how to go about researching, evaluating, and buying equipment. It's pretty dense material, but perhaps it will save you some time, money, and costly mistakes.

Chapter 3 is the core of the book. It's a group of thirty case studies, in which I partially or wholly reconstruct illustrations within each of the main categories of my work:

charts, maps, classifications, and technical diagrams. We focus on both the key technical aspects and the most important design considerations of each image.

I hope that when you see the various things you can do with state-of-the-art illustration software—in far less time, generally, than it takes to do them using traditional tools and methods—you'll be tempted to enter the world of electronic design, at least for an exploratory visit.

The final chapter discusses one of the most vexing problems an active computer illustrator faces: the matter of managing one's hundreds or thousands of stored images. We briefly look at some new "visual database" software programs which let us catalog and index files, so that when you need an image, you can quickly find and retrieve it.

CHAPTER

1.

Gallery

*B*efore we get into the main section of the book, Chapter 3, "Case Studies," I'd like to present a variety of illustrations I've done on the Macintosh, using some of the best illustration and painting programs.

This Gallery is organized into two-page spreads, each of which focuses on an important category of illustrations: pie charts, bar charts, fever charts, maps and icons, illustrations, and diagrams.

I hope that this short showcase will give you some idea of the effects that an illustrator can achieve with these wonderful electronic tools (and I've by no means done everything that can be done with these programs).

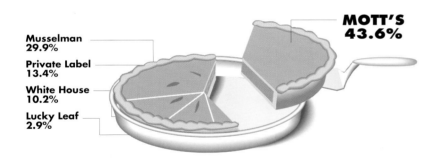

PIE CHARTS: The pie chart is ideal for showing percentage breakdowns.

ILLUSTRATIONS: Illustrations commonly employ symbols, analogies, and, as in this case, metaphors.

BAR CHARTS: Bar sharts show comparative quantities or proportions.

FEVER CHARTS: The familiar jagged line of a fever chart, which shows changes over time.

DIAGRAMS: A diagram simplifies a structure or a process down to its essentials.

MAPS/ICONS: The world-apple, both an icon and a map, symbolizes global harmony—or the hope for it.

Pie Charts

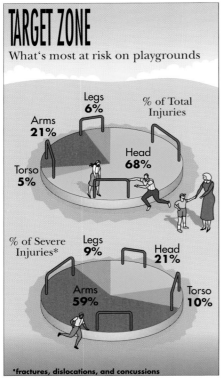

TARGET ZONE

What's most at risk on playgrounds

Legs 6%
Arms 21%
% of Total Injuries
Head 68%
Torso 5%

% of Severe Injuries*
Legs 9%
Head 21%
Arms 59%
Torso 10%

*fractures, dislocations, and concussions

1. The two merry-go-rounds show the likelihood of body parts to be injured in a playground accident.

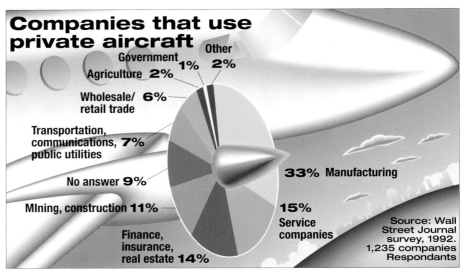

Companies that use private aircraft

Government 1%
Other 2%
Agriculture 2%
Wholesale/ retail trade 6%
Transportation, communications, public utilities 7%
No answer 9%
Mining, construction 11%
Finance, insurance, real estate 14%
33% Manufacturing
15% Service companies

Source: Wall Street Journal survey, 1992. 1,235 companies Respondants

2. This chart from Beechcraft Business News shows the percentages of companies in different industries that use private planes. The whir-blur of a spinning propeller seemed an unusually good visual vehicle for the pie.

40%

of all Americans will be involved in an alcohol related car accident in their lifetime, according to the U.S. Department of Transportation.

40%

3. This pie, from a Whittle Communications booklet on substance abuse, uses the steering wheel to show the 40 per cent of Americans who will be involved in an alcohol-related car accident in their lifetimes.

4. The pedestal slice rising from this 3-D pie dramatizes the 25 per cent of families who have a problem with substance abuse.

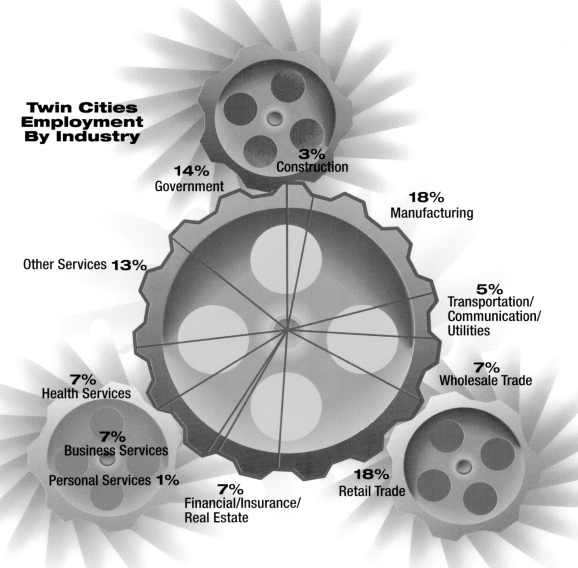

Twin Cities Employment By Industry

3% Construction

14% Government

18% Manufacturing

Other Services 13%

5% Transportation/ Communication/ Utilities

7% Health Services

7% Wholesale Trade

7% Business Services

Personal Services 1%

18% Retail Trade

7% Financial/Insurance/ Real Estate

Source: Minnesota Department of Jobs and Training, "Minnestoa Labor Market Review," August, 1993.

5. The pie chart is the center gear in this illustration portraying employment by industry in Minnesota's Twin Cities.

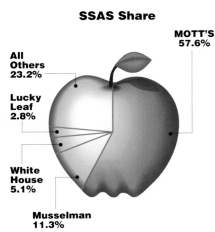

SSAS Share

MOTT'S 57.6%

All Others 23.2%

Lucky Leaf 2.8%

White House 5.1%

Musselman 11.3%

6. This apple pie shows the market shares of apple sauce companies.

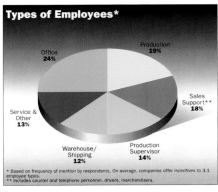

Types of Employees*

Office 24%

Production 19%

Sales Support** 18%

Service & Other 13%

Warehouse/ Shipping 12%

Production Supervisor 14%

* Based on frequency of mention by respondents. On average, companies offer incentives to 3.1 employee types.
** Includes counter and telephone personnel, drivers, merchandisers.

7. A quintessential pie chart, one that Ross Perot would be proud of. This one shows workers broken down by occupations in Georgia.

Who Sells What

How far can you get these days with a shoestring and a smile? In 1990, 4.7 million direct sales representatives sold $11.82 billion worth of merchandise in this country. A whopping 88.4 percent of those salespeople were female. Here's what they sold:

Services/ other 6.1%

Leisure/ educational products 11.9%

Home/Family care products 46.9%

Personal care products 35.1%

8. A breakdown of percentage of sales accounted for by different product groups.

Bar Charts

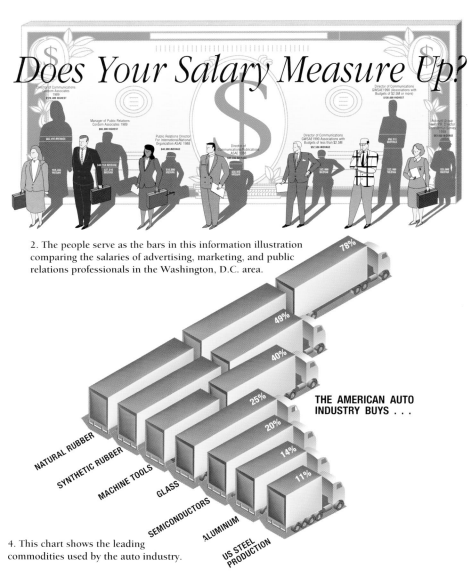

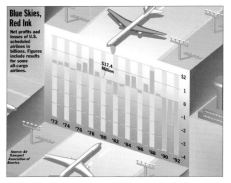

1. In this chart showing airline profitability over a 10-year span, the huge hangar door is the plane for the bars.

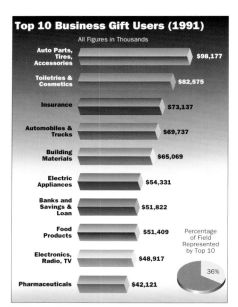

3. The top 10 business-gift-giving industries are displayed in this spacious, colorful bar chart. I liked the colors of these bars so much that I've actually used this illustration a number of times as a color palette for other illustrations. It's totally visual: unlike a color dialog box, in which you have to specify your colors, with this "palette" I just click on whichever color I want and it's selected. If you're like me and dislike entering values in dialog boxes, you may want to try something like this.

2. The people serve as the bars in this information illustration comparing the salaries of advertising, marketing, and public relations professionals in the Washington, D.C. area.

4. This chart shows the leading commodities used by the auto industry.

5. Ski poles formed the sides of the bars in this chart for an article on spending for ski apparel, equipment, and accessories.

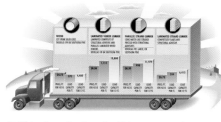

6. This chart for Popular Science magazine showed both prices and load capacity for four categories of wood composites.

7. The ascending slabs in this chart represent the per-family tax burdens in each state.

8. I used a basketball backboard to carry 50 miniature bar charts. They ranked the states according to the percentage of college basketball players who didn't graduate.

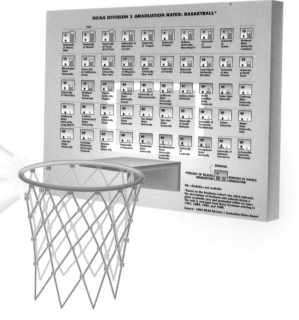

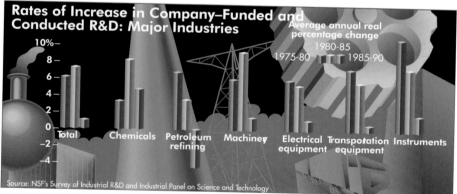

9. This appeared in an engineering trade association magazine.

10. The leading causes of death are the subject of the bars which are worn by the heart (heart disease is the number one cause).

Fever Charts

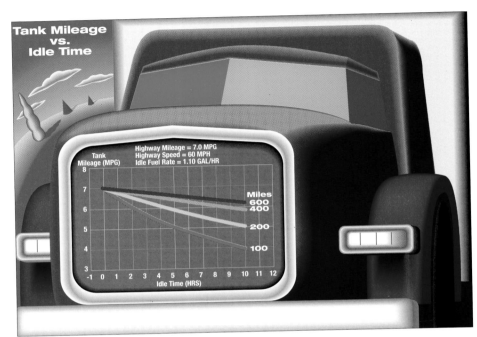

1. This chart shows the trends in capital expenditures for 5-year periods by the German chemical industry.

2. I had to diagram the effects of truck idling time on gas mileage and on the number of miles between overhauls. For the visual vehicles I tried to use obvious symbols in appealing ways: the truck grille, odometers, highway and ramps.

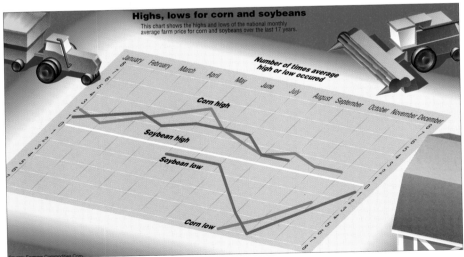

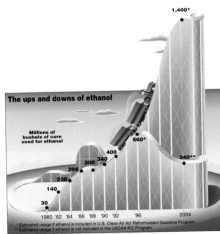

3. A compound fever chart, showing two measurements (high and low prices) for two commodities (corn and soybeans) over a 17-year span.

4. The steep growth projected for the use of corn to make methanol is dramatized by making the chart line the track of a towering roller coaster.

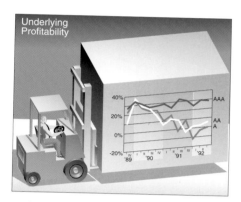

Underlying Profitability

5. This fever chart for the International Monetary Fund's journal *Finance and Development* shows the profitability of companies with various bond ratings.

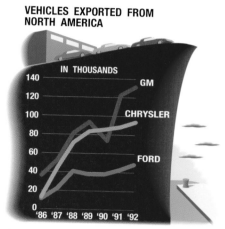

VEHICLES EXPORTED FROM NORTH AMERICA

6. For this chart showing the growth in exports of U.S. cars, I used the side of a ship's hull.

7. A house under construction is the plane for a chart for a Champion International newsletter.

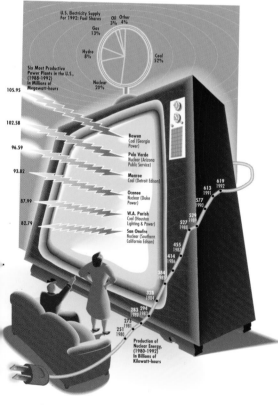

8. A hybrid of bar chart, fever, and pie chart, showing various statistics about electricity supply and demand.

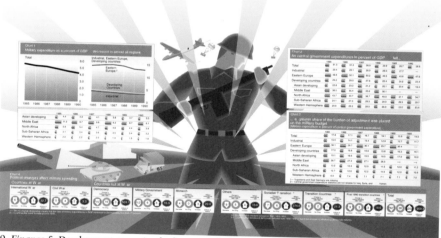

9. *Finance & Development* magazine had a great deal of information that had to be presented clearly in one illustration. It actually contains three types of statistical graphics: fever charts (Chart 1), bar charts (the horizontal bars in Charts 1-3 and the ten components of Chart 4), and tables (the numerical columns in Charts 1-3).

Maps
and
Icons

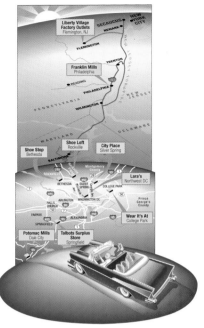

1. This is a map of the "best" outlet shopping malls in the Washington-New York megalopolois.

2. I extended a U.S. map into 3-D and put the crushing burden of the resulting slab on an AIDS patient. The data are AIDS rates per 100,000 population.

NETWORKS

3. This spherical map, done for Geotek Industries, Inc., pinpoints the location of the cities which are designated to be activated under the "GEONET" TM telecommunications system.

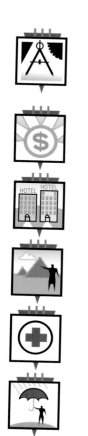

5. This map of the mall area in Washington, D.C., had to clearly show a great deal of information.

7. I did these four symbols for an article on various aspects of technical training.

8. I did a set of bar charts to show key economic indicators. They were pretty basic, so I added this set of icons to anchor the bars, to symbolize each topic, and to add visual interest.

4. I did a large U.S. map in which I had to show the most promising job areas for each state. It would have been a for-bidding graphic if text had been used to indicate the occupations. Icons were the way to make the information visi-ble at a glance. (A key to the occupa-tions represented by the icons appeared at the bottom of the illustration.)

6. A map icon for an article on international shipping.

9. I used an old-fashioned ticker tape machine for an article on stock prices.

10. This livened up an article on technology companies in Georgia.

11. This schematic map shows the layout of the upper and lower levels of the Baltimore-Washington International Airport.

Illustrations

1. This illustration was for an *Aldus Magazine* article on the problem of how to get PC diskettes translated into Macintosh format.

2. From an article on how lawyers are chosen: why some are picked and others aren't.

3. A *Washington Post* article discussed problems a computer network faces.

4. This illustration shows a trainer overseeing a worker, with the dollar sign looming overhead—for an article on companies that try to save money in training programs.

5. A training journal did an article which classified technical troubleshooters into three types. This illustration was for the "testers" category.

6. From a computer magazine article on how to get foreign fonts into the Aldus PageMaker program.

7. This illlustration symbolizes the one in four families who have an alcohol abuse problem.

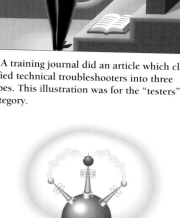

8. This image, reminiscent of a transformation chamber in an old Frankenstein movie, was used as a metaphor for the "mysterious" process by which PageMaker 5.0 translated a document formatted in the 4.0 version.

10. This was for an article on interactive teaching programs of the future.

9. Another article in *Aldus Magazine* explained why laser printer pages were coming out with the tops of images cropped.

Diagrams

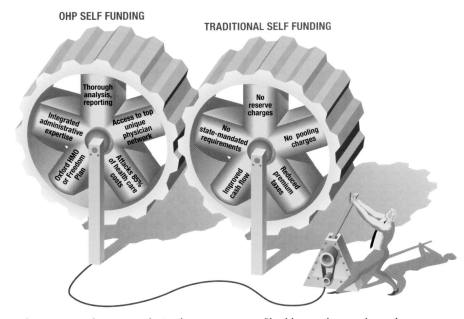

OHP SELF FUNDING

TRADITIONAL SELF FUNDING

1. This illustration of a commercial airliner exchanging signals with the Gannett Building in Rosslyn, Va., via a link with a 26,000-mile-high communication satellite, shows the basic dynamic of USA Today's Sky Radio system.

2. The gears were chosen to analogize the way two types of health care plans mesh together.

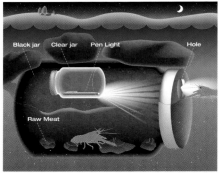

3. A very simple, literal diagram. The headline says it all.

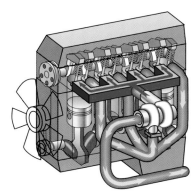

4. This Anheuser-Busch ad aims to show how quickly Budweiser trucks hit the road after an order comes in.

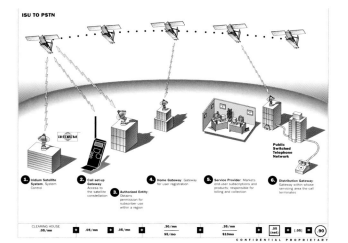

5. A diagram portraying the operation of Motorola Corp.'s Iridium system.

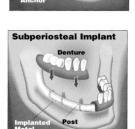

6. These illustrations, done for *Prevention* magazine, show the two most common procedures for implanting false teeth.

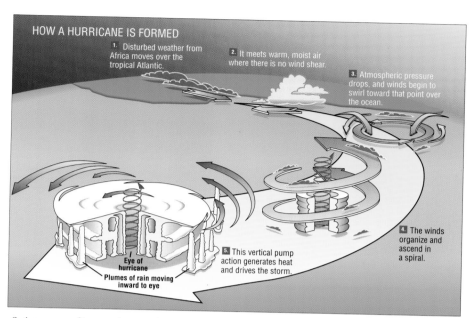

HOW A HURRICANE IS FORMED

1. Disturbed weather from Africa moves over the tropical Atlantic.

2. It meets warm, moist air where there is no wind shear.

3. Atmospheric pressure drops, and winds begin to swirl toward that point over the ocean.

4. The winds organize and ascend in a spiral.

5. This vertical pump action generates heat and drives the storm.

Eye of hurricane

Plumes of rain moving inward to eye

8. A sequence diagram showing the key stages in the formation of a hurricane.

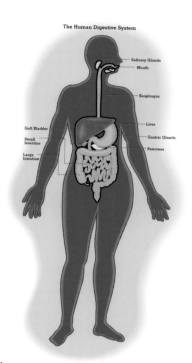

The Human Digestive System

Salivary Glands
Mouth
Esophogus
Liver
Gall Bladder
Gastric Glands
Small Intestine
Pancreas
Large Intestine

7. The components of the digestive system. For a science textbook.

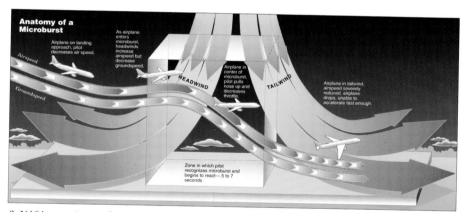

Anatomy of a Microburst

Airplane on landing approach, pilot decreases air speed.

As airplane enters microburst, headwinds increase airspeed but decrease groundspeed.

Airplane in center of microburst, pilot pulls nose up and decreases throttle.

Airplane in tailwind, airspeed severely reduced, airplane drops, unable to accelerate fast enough.

Airspeed
Groundspeed
HEADWIND
TAILWIND

Zone in which pilot recognizes microburst and begins to react—.5 to 7 seconds.

9. NASA commissioned me to do this illustration of the potentially disastrous effects of a type of air pocket, a microburst, on airplanes trying to land—and a pilot's very short cube of opportunity for reacting. A technical diagram portraying forces and dynamics.

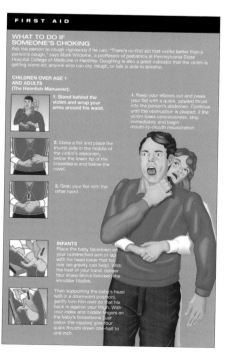

10. How to stop someone from choking. A diagram illustrating the Heimlich maneuver.

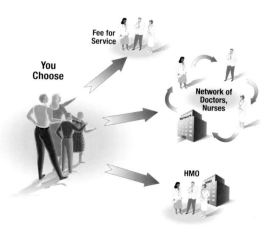

Fee for Service

You Choose

Network of Doctors, Nurses

HMO

11. A diagram for a pamphlet for the White House explaining the key features of President Clinton's health care plan. This graphic attempts to show that Americans will keep their right to choose their own health care providers.

CHAPTER

2.

Setting Up An Electronic Studio

1. A long view of my studio.

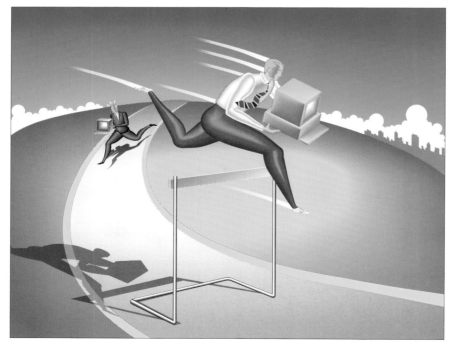

Clearing the Hardware and Software Hurdles

An illustrator who wants to come to computer-based design from a traditional set-up is likely to feel intimidated by all the information she has to digest and by all the complicated decisions she has to make:

What hardware do I need to get? From whom should I buy it? How much memory will I need to work with images, and to store them? What illustration software should I get? What other types of programs will I need?

Take heart. Everyone else feels the same way when they start out—and later, as they "upgrade" their systems, and upgrade again and again. Sometimes I dream of a time when all software is perfect and new versions just aren't happening anymore. Sometimes I'm profoundly tired of 3.0's and 5.1's, and never want to see another "new feature." (Well, there are a few I'd like to see.)

In this chapter I tell you about my stuff, the hardware and software components of my system. I also note the areas where my equipment is less than ideal at the moment (these situations will have been remedied, I hope, by the time this book comes out). And I tell you what I would like to get, given that my wife and I are a two-person show and our treasury is not a mint. Let's begin, though with a description and photographs of my studio.

2. At one end of the studio is a comfortable place for having conferences, or just being lazy.

THE STUDIO LAYOUT

I work in the lower level of my home. Part of the lower level is the design studio of my four young daughters, and the other half is mine (I hope they don't plan to expand).

It's a long, ample 42' x 12' workspace with white walls (1) and no windows (outside light causes glare), and adjustable track lighting. I highly recommend tracks: you can slide the light canisters and direct them any way you want; you can also add light canisters to the track. It's nice, warm light.

At one end is a comfortable place for conferences (2). At the other end are my drafting table, file cabinets, and laser printer (1). In the middle, where I spend most of my time, is my hardware system: two Macintoshes, three terminals, keyboards, various disk drives, modem, fax machine, and phones (4).

I sit with all this stuff within arm's reach, which I think is very important. The one thing I can't reach or easily slide my chair to is my laser printer. Sometimes I think, well, let's get the printer over here, too. Then I'll have total sit-down access. On the other hand, it does give me an excuse to get up and stretch my legs (often I'm cranking away at the Mac so intently that I go two or even three hours without standing up).

My drafting table, which I still use for airbrushing and for laying out multiple-illustration projects, is a top-of-the-line Neolt Poker Architetto (3).

For storage I have two 4-drawer file cabinets, which are full of reference clippings I've saved over the years, organized by major subjects; a 4-drawer lateral file for storing printed electronic works and original non-electronic art; and six large Bankers' Boxes, in which I keep all my project files.

If there are two rules for setting up a studio, they must be these: You can't have too much space, and you can't have too much storage. In planning my studio in 1986, I tried to anticipate my growing space needs to accommodate my expanding business; yet already the nooks and crannies are all starting to fill up. The same for storage. If you're successful, you won't believe the file space you'll

need to store the paperwork from your hundreds and then thousands of illustration projects.

(The matter of electronic storage is another can of worms, and is discussed below under "Hardware," and in Chapter 4.)

HARDWARE

We might as well mention the painful part first. To work as a serious computer illustrator—to run the sophisticated, memory-devouring programs you'll need to produce complex color image files—requires a powerful and expensive system. The total cost of the equipment listed above, if purchased at this date (Spring 1994), would be somewhere around $19,000. Of course, you might spend several thousand more, or less.

Keep in mind that this is not a checklist of equipment to go out and buy. What are important are the performance capabilities of the different components. They're standards that meet my current needs.

But in most cases you have a choice of manufacturers and resellers, who provide different packages, prices, and levels of customer service. Also, many of the items and capabilities I list will probably be superseded by newer and better things—by the time this book comes out.

So far as I know, I'm with it in electronic design circles as of Spring 1994. But I can't put too much emphasis on my principal recom-

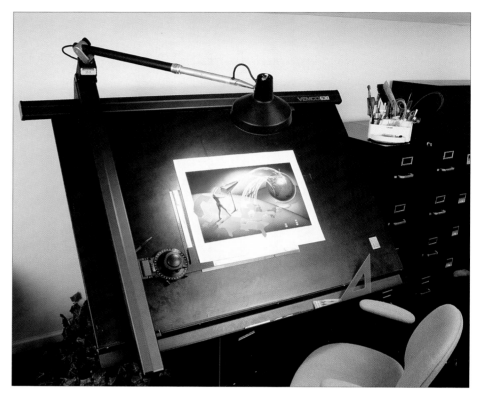

3. My Neolt drafting table. I still use it for airbrushing and for laying out projects with multiple illustrations.

mendation: that if you are a novice computer user and buyer, you should find a hip and reliable dealer who can translate your needs into an economical system that gives you the capabilities you need, and can reasonably foresee yourself needing for a year or two—but not a lot more than that.

(An excellent and thorough, although dated (1989) discussion of the crucial considerations and pitfalls you need to consider in planning and purchasing your equipment is Chapter 2, "Tools of the Trade," in *Getting Started in Computer Graphics,* by Gary Olsen. Very highly recommended.)

MY SYSTEM:

1) Computers:
—Macintosh Quadra 950, 72 megabytes RAM, with Radius Rocket accelerator, 33 MHz, System 7 operating system
—Macintosh IIx, 32 megabytes RAM, with Radius Rocket accelerator, 33 MHz. System 7 operating system
—Macintosh Centris 610, 24 megabytes RAM. System 7 operating system
(In the photos you may notice a Mac Plus. After the photos were taken, this was replaced by the Centris and the Quadra. I still use the trusty Plus for word crunching.)

2) Monitors:
—small monitor: 13" Sony color multimedia monitor, multi-sync, 24-bit accelerator card
—medium sized monitors, 2—17" monitors that run off the internal video and accelerator card
—large monitor: 19" Sony color monitor with 8-bit card (unaccelerated)

3) Keyboard: Apple Extended Keyboard

4) Printer: GCC SelectPress 600 laser printer, 600 dpi, black-and-white, 11" x 17," with 80 megabyte internal hard drive

5) Fax: Sharp, 11" x 17," outputting to 8" x 11," with 16 shades of gray

6) Electronic tablet: Wacom digitizing tablets with stylus

7) Modem: Practical Peripherals 9600 baud, V-dot 32

8) Scanner: Lightning 300 dpi, black-and-white, hand-held scanner, with Lightning Scan software

9) Networking hardware: Ethernet cards and cables

10) Hard disk drive (internal):
—Macintosh Quadra 950: Raven 1 gigabyte array.
—Macintosh IIx: Quantum 425 megabyte.
—Macintosh Centris 610: 230 megabyte drive

11) External storage devices:
—Syquest drives with 44/88 megabyte Syquest disks
—Infinity magneto-optical drive with 128 megabyte 3.5" disks
—MicroNet CD-ROM drive and Apple CD-ROM drives, with 650-megabyte read-only CD's
—Soon to come: 2-gigabyte external drive, plus 3-8 gigabyte erasable DAT drive for automatic overnight backup

●　●　●　●　●

My primary computer is a Macintosh Quadra 950, with 72 megabytes of RAM. With its Radius Rocket accelerator card, 24 megabytes of RAM, it also operates at 33 Megahertz. You'll want this much RAM and speed when you're involved in implementing your graphic instructions, and the time required to redraw your image on the screen.

The Quadra's have a new architecture that crunches data more efficiently, and, as you'll quickly learn, speed is the name of the game.

My 72-megabyte setup is just right when I'm working with multi-megabyte images, especially when I have fonts loaded. Speed junkies need to have 128 megs. Unfortunately, a megabyte of RAM is expensive, currently costing about $40, when you buy it as 4-megabyte chips. I'd recommend starting with at least 32 megs, and adding more as you need it. My other computers, a Mac IIx and the Centris 610, are

4. A wide-angle shot of my system. Everything except the laser printer is within arm's reach.

doing serious illustration work, because of the huge RAM demands of the software and your created images, the processing complexity used for rendering 3-D animations, running print jobs, and less demanding graphic, word processing, and desktop publishing.

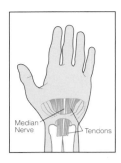

Median Nerve   Tendons

My **monitors** are the other very expensive part of my system (5). You can't skimp on them, though; not if you want to make a living as an illustrator. My small one, on which I do most of my work, is a 13" Sony multimedia, multisync monitor. It has a 24-bit accelerator card which I installed separately. The card greatly speeds up screen redrawing time and I view it as absolutely essential.

The 17" medium-sized monitors, a SuperMatch and an NEC, are good workhorses for graphics work, with their 24-bit accelerated card and internal video.

The large monitor is a 19" color Sony, unaccelerated, with a screen resolution of 1024 by 768 pixels. It's better for displaying large images, which is an important consideration when a client comes to visit. On this screen you can also display two illustration pages in programs like QuarkXPress or FreeHand.

One thing I would like for all the monitors, but can't yet afford, is a color calibrator. A calibrator is a curious contraption with something like a suction cup that attaches to your screen. What it does is make the screen colors the same as your output colors—those you designate with your software, the ones you want to see in the final printed piece. It's expensive, currently running $5-6,000, but in the long run will pay for itself because, in most cases, you will no longer have to order expensive Cromalin proofs.

5. These are my two monitors, both from Sony. The smaller one, 13", has a 24-bit accelerator card which quickly redraws the screen. The larger monitor, 19", is used for displaying large images, and also for keeping my illustration palettes in view.

I recommend that you get two monitors, if you can afford it. The primary reason is that you can keep all your illustration setups and controls—color palettes, layers palettes, style palettes, airbrush settings boxes, etc.—in view, without hogging up the screen you're drawing on.

My **printer** is a GCC SelectPress 600 dpi laser printer. It's more expensive than a 300 dpi printer, but the extra resolution is worth having, as is the 11" by 17" output. I'd like eventually to buy a color laser printer—it would save much of the time and expense in working with a service bureau—but at present the cost is a little prohibitive.

The rest of the hardware equipment—fax, digitizing tablet and stylus, modem, scanner, and networking hardware—is comparatively simpler to shop for. However, as with the computer, monitor, storage devices, and printer, I recommend getting expert advice, both from reviews in publications like *MacUser,* and from knowledgeable people at dealers.

THE PROBLEM OF STORAGE
In the old days (before 1988 or 1989) a computer artist or illustrator could get by on less than a hundred megabytes of hard disk storage for his application software and his image files. I did—when I got my Mac IIx in 1988 it came with an

80mb hard drive. This was enough storage for a while—a short while.

Soon it began to fill up. Every time one of my drawing, painting, and other programs was updated, it seemed to need several hundred thousand more bytes just to run, and the image files it generated grew and grew.

When one particular program (which shall remain nameless) came out with a hot new souped-up version, my image sizes jumped 30 to 40 percent overnight!

As a storage device, such as a hard disk drive, starts to get full, it slows down dramatically. The system has to search around in every digital nook and cranny for empty space big enough to store your newest creation. And your system becomes prone to crashes, which can be anything from annoying to disastrous.

I think that nowadays (as of this writing, in Spring 1994), a professional illustrator probably shouldn't consider getting a hard disk drive with a capacity of less than 400 megabytes. Believe me, if you are a passing fair success, your disk is going to fill up at a pace that will have you gasping.

As I've grown busier and busier and the image files have gotten bigger and bigger, I find that *each year* I'm generating much more than 425 megabytes of illustrations and other files that have to be stored. Where do I put it all? I'm an illustrator, not a warehouser.

SYQUEST'S AND INFINITY'S AND A MULTI-GIGABYTE MONSTER

I've found several options for external storage. Each has its trade-offs in terms of portability and price. Let's briefly look at them, in what I imagine would be the order in which you'd need them.

First, you'll need an easily portable external storage disk and drive. There will be many occasions when you'll be sending—or taking in person—illustration files that are simply massive: multi-megabyte, far too large to load onto a 1.4 meg diskette. Since you'll probably be routing these monster graphic files around from your studio to a service bureau or a client and back, you will want a disk that is light, relatively cheap, and durable, and has high capacity.

For me, that disk is the **SyQuest**. It holds 88 megabytes and is roughly the size of a compact disc. It's become an industry standard and, consequentially, various companies (including SyQuest) make the disks and drives. They're all compatible and of good quality; shop around. For a larger capacity storage medium that is about the same size as a SyQuest, although more expensive for both drive and disk, consider **magneto-optical** drives. I use a PLI Infinity drive. The Infinity disks are only 3.5 inches square, but they store 128 megabytes of stuff—from 30 to 300 files. And they have a very long life for disks: 15 years.

CD-ROM: THE DIGITAL MUSEUM

A third type of external memory system has much more capacity than

6. Almost all of my electronic equipment, except for the laser printer, is within arm's reach.

either the SyQuest or the magneto-optical systems, but is read-only: **CD-ROM** (compact disc, read-only memory). CD-ROM's are superlative for storing extremely high density images such as photographs, works of art, or your own created images (it is now possible to record your own CD's for only about $15-$20 per image).

The tradeoff is that a CD-ROM, like a diamond, is essentially forever. You can't go into it, download an image, work on it, and then put it back into the disk. In other words, you can change an image from a CD-ROM, but as soon as you do, you have to put it somewhere else, like a hard drive or a SyQuest. Nevertheless, with its capacity of 550-650 megabytes per disk, you should consider buying a CD-ROM drive so that you can have access to the growing number of high-resolution photographic and cartographic archives available on this format.

(For a reference to a forthcoming, exciting set of CD-ROM's which will provide high-quality digitized aerial photographs of the entire U.S., see the discussion "A Map of the Mall" in chapter 3 (p. 86) of this book.)

INTO THE MAGNITUDE OF GIGABYTES

Let's pause briefly and do a rough inventory of megabytes. My image armamentarium now occupies almost my entire 425 megabyte hard drive, plus nearly two dozen Syquest disks at 44 megs per, plus 15-20 Infinity optical disks at 128 megs. I

have somewhere between three and four *gigabytes* of images stored on various internal and external devices—not even counting my CD-ROM's! A decade or so ago, this much digital territory would have been the province of a Department of Defense supercomputer facility. And now it's all in Dale's studio.

As I write this, in Spring 1994, I feel that I'm at a critical juncture: I must quit thinking in terms of storing megabytes, and start thinking—routinely—in terms of storing gigabytes. A "gig" is 1,000 megabytes. You, as a budding electronic illustrator, may as well make up your mind to think about storing gigs from the outset; then you'll have sidestepped digital culture shock.

What we'll both need to have is a multi-gigabyte external hard drive. Currently there are 1-gigabyte and 2-gigabyte drives on the market; I'd recommend getting the bigger one, because you'll probably end up needing it eventually.

This big drive not only will let me store everything I have to store; it also will store it in *one place*. This is very important. When you have things stored all over the place—in internal hard disks, and external SyQuest and Infinity optical disks, for example—it makes for a long day when you're trying to find a particular image file.

A MASTER BACKUP SYSTEM

But it's not enough just to have a centralized storage system for your

images and other files. You also need to back them up—make separately-located copies of them—regularly, preferably at the end of each work-day. There are many kinds of backup strategies you can use. The most common practice, which I still follow myself, is to copy files onto diskettes or high-capacity disks such as the SyQuest and Infinity disks that I described above.

A much better setup, however, one I plan to install soon, is a digital audio tape (DAT) system connected to one of my Macs. This "master Mac" will have software that will instruct it to query each of my storage units (the big 2-gigabyte drive in the future; the internal hard drive and external disk drives at present).

It will ask each of the storage devices which files are new and which have been changed in any way since the last query (update), probably the night before. Then, using something called ADSP (AppleTalk Data Stream Protocol), the master Mac sends all the files to be updated to the tape drive, which copies them.

Whatever backup method you use, you have to keep to it faithfully—unless you are the type of person who can go to bed and sleep, knowing that if one of your disks crashes or fails, many precious images, representing long, arduous work sessions, may be lost forever. I don't have that kind of cavalier, even irresponsible attitude; I can't afford to lose work.

7. It's good to allow yourself enough space to expand. For example I'm starting to establish a second power workstation. The Macintosh Plus has been replaced by a newer Mac Centris and Quadra 950.

So, a multi-gigabyte drive and a DAT backup system will solve one aspect—the hardware part— of the critical problem of managing your image information system. The other part of the puzzle has to do with indexing your files, and choosing the software that lets you organize your files into an image database, so that you can search it powerfully and quickly to find the file you're after. This part of the problem will be discussed in detail in Chapter 4, "Image Management."

SOFTWARE

The graphic software arena is becoming increasingly competitive. Where five or six years ago each niche was dominated by an unchallenged kingpin program, nowadays there's an intense race to be the first out with the next set of sea changes. It's difficult for an electronic illustra-

tor, especially one new to the field, to know which programs are best suited for handling specific tasks. Probably the sanest way to proceed is to build a set of core programs, then try to evaluate—in a hands-on way, if possible—each updated version of that program and its chief competitors, as they're released. This way, you'll maintain an up-to-date awareness of current capabilities which will let you know whether you should upgrade, or switch.

CORE ILLUSTRATION SOFTWARE

I recommend that a newly-electronic illustrator begin building his software library by choosing at least one program in each of the following "big four" categories:

A) **Drawing programs:** Aldus' *FreeHand;* Adobe Systems' *Illustrator;* Denebe Software's *Canvas*

B) **Paint and image-enhancement programs:** Adobe Systems' *Photoshop;* Fractal Design's *Painter* and *Color Studio*

C) **3-D modeling, rendering, and animation programs:** Electric Image Inc.'s *Electric Image;* Specular International's *Infini-D;* Adobe Systems' *Dimensions;* MacroMedia's *Macromind Director, Swivel 3D,* and *MacroModel;* Strata Inc.'s *StrataVISION*

D) **Page layout programs:** Quark Inc.'s *QuarkXPress;* Aldus' *PageMaker*

These are all top-class programs. They all work together well; all are compatible with the PostScript page description language (so that your complex graphics can be printed); and all receive regular and major updates for the Macintosh. You may start out not needing software in one of the categories—you have no intention of getting into 3-D right away, for example—so you need to do some soul-searching concerning the style or styles of illustration you want to work in, at least at the beginning.

On the one hand is the cost of buying a bunch of programs. On the other hand, you don't want to rein yourself in, constrain yourself from doing images in certain ways because you don't have the appropriate type of software— and because doing the image with the software you do have would take so long that you'd get burned out, or not make money, or both. (For a case study on this matter, see the discussions: "The Sun" and "The Solar Darkroom," on pages 34 and 38, respectively.)

The other software you'll need falls into several categories, of which the specific programs in the following listing are only examples of the many fine programs in each class:

—**Word processing:** Microsoft Corp.'s *Word*; WordPerfect Corp.'s *WordPerfect*

—**Font software:** Altsys' *Fontographer*; Adobe Systems' *Super ATM*; Fifth Generation Systems' *Suitcase*

—**Image management programs:** Aldus' *Fetch*; Kodak's *Shoebox*; MacApp's *Lightbox*

—**Spreadsheets:** Microsoft's *Excel*

—**Communications/modem software:** Software Ventures Corp.'s *MicroPhone*

—**File compression:** Aladdin Systems' *StuffIt*; Salient's *Disk Doubler*

—**File rescue:** *Norton Utilities* — memory extension (virtual memory); Connectix Corp.'s *Maxima*

Recently I drew a set of illustrations showing correct and incorrect positions for sitting at a computer. You've seen them running along the tops of the pages in this chapter. Now let's run through them.

The advice from the office ergonomic experts might be put in a nutshell as: Don't be tight; sit upright. The idea is to sit in a way that lets you be comfortable for long sittings. And you won't be comfortable for long if the muscles in your lower back, neck, wrists, or other areas get tight and strained.

The first requirement is a good chair, one with a natural curve that supports the lumbar area of the lower back. This chair should let you sit with the line of your spine at an angle somewhere in the range of 93 to 111 degrees to a horizontal plane.

Figures 1 and 2 show a person sitting in a suitable chair in a good posture. His eyes are just slightly higher than the center of his screen, and he's neither too close nor too far away. The other diagrams (3-6) show our terminal man in less than ideal positions. If you sit too close, you'll ruin your eyesight and strain your upper back and neck (3). Too low and you put too much burden on your wrist muscles to support your forearms (4); this is a primary cause of carpal tunnel syndrome, a painful and mobility-limiting wrist disorder.

Sitting too high (5) or at an angle to your terminal (6) also strain your eyesight or certain muscle groups.

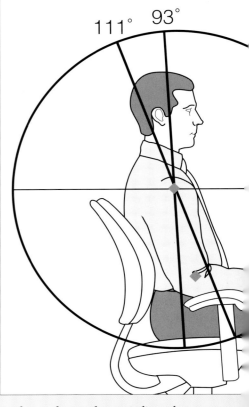

1. The numbers in degrees indicate the recommended range for the angle of the spine (relative to a horizontal plane).

2. Sitting in a good chair in an ideal position.

4. Don't sit so low that your elbows are lower than your keyboard; this is a surefire way to strain your wrists and perhaps develop carpal tunnel syndrome.

3. A good way to strain your eyes, your neck, and your back is to sit too close to your terminal or lean forward to it from your chair.

5, 6. Sitting too high, or at an angle to your monitor, also often cause aches and strains.

CHAPTER
3.

Case Studies

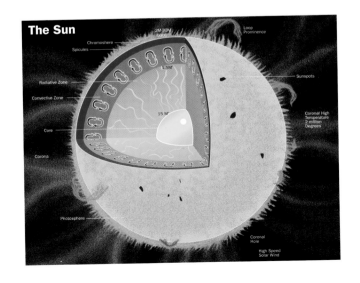

A How-To Primer on Information Illustration

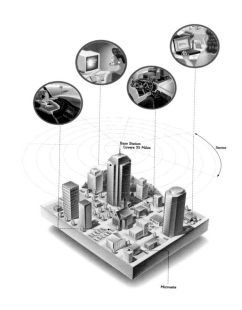

I n the "Gallery" chapter, I showed you examples of the kinds of work upon which I've built my success and reputation. Now let's take some of my illustrations and reconstruct them. Let's see just how they evolved.

For the most part, we won't do complete step-by-step re-creations, but instead focus on the most interesting technical or design aspects of a piece. Usually we'll start at the thumbnail stage and look at the different ideas I had for an illustration. We'll also recount the dialogue with the client, and consider the factors that led to the choice of the final conception.

Then we'll move to the Macintosh and start building up the illustration. We'll draw lines and render shapes, organize them on layers, apply colors and fills and blends, stretch and skew and flip objects, work with type, do electronic filtering and air-brushing, make 3-D objects out of 2-D images, construct 3-point perspectives, clone things, power-duplicate things, and do many other things that modern illustration software enables you to do.

But we won't just be interested in techniques. We'll place equal em-phasis on the question of how I choose the visual vehicles to illustrate various types of information. We'll look at situations in which a bar chart, or a pie chart, or a "fever chart," are appropriate to handle statistical data. We'll consider the problems involved in planning a complex technical diagram. We'll take several close looks at maps, and how I try to make them clear and appealing. That's really the challenge most of the time: to take a bunch of facts, and make them clear, instantly graspable, and visually engaging.

Finally, in a number of cases, we'll see how two or three different software programs are used to create one illustration, how two kinds of software with fundamentally different features can powerfully complement each other, and how easily we can move our illustration files around among the different programs.

The aim of this chapter is neither to show you a lot of exhaustive step-by-step technical scenarios, nor to be a substitute for user manuals, tutorials, and a great deal of practice. Rather, I hope that these discussions will show you many of the stunning effects that the computer illustrator has at his fingertips, and perhaps entice you to enter this magical world of vectors, pixels, toolboxes, and mice.

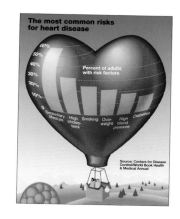

The Sun

The Star With the Dithered Spicules

I've done several things for NASA that I count among my best efforts in drawing technical diagrams. This job was no exception.

The Orbiting Solar Laboratory—"Our Window on the Sun"—was to be NASA's prime solar research mission for the 1990's. In order to educate the public and, perhaps more importantly, to enlist the support of Congress, the agency was preparing a booklet the size of an annual report, with an annual report's showcase quality printing, photography, and illustrations.

I was commissioned to do the illustrations, and one of the focal ones was to be a picture of the sun, showing its surface, off-surface phenomena, and a cutaway of its interior furnace (1).

In order to construct this complex illustration, I needed, among many other things, to create several airbrush-like textures, to render four surface and above-surface features of the sun that are turbulent and dynamic, full of fiery energy that is ever on the verge of exploding: the surface, the corona, the loop prominences, and the spicules (1).

I wanted to achieve a painterly style with the textures. Each of them had to simulate continuous tone, each had to print transparently over the surfaces or backgrounds behind

CLIENT: NASA
TIME: 16 hours
SIZE: 500k
PROGRAM: FreeHand

> ❝Each of the textures had to simulate continuous tone, and each had to print transparently over the surfaces or backgrounds behind them.❞

them, and each had to convey an impression of disturbing, unsettled heat energy.

There are several techniques an illustrator can use to create textures like these. First, you can employ electronic blending tools such as FreeHand's "blend" feature. Or you can airbrush a texture and then import it into FreeHand as a PICT file, which is line art, or as a TIFF file, which is a halftone.

Let's look at the corona, the purple "sprays" encircling the sun and extending far out into space (2). They had to have an ethereal, flowing look and had to be transparent so that the black background of space would show through the interstices of the purple textures.

It would have been possible to create the corona "all-electronically," using FreeHand's blend tool. However, it wouldn't have been practical. Each of the twenty or so coronal sprays would have had to be a separate blend, which would have been very time-consuming. The same problem would apply to the creation of the other textures.

2. Close-up of one the coronal sprays, showing the randomlike pattern of dots produced by a dither.

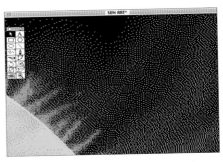

3. Close-up of dither patterns for the sun's surface, spicules, and corona.

4. Loop prominences: pencil art ready to be scanned by ThunderWorks.

I chose to airbrush the coronal sprays, scan the art, and import it into FreeHand as halftone TIFF's. Once I made this decision, the techniques for creating the other three textures was made as well—they would also be hand-drawn and scanned in. The four textures would overlap in various places on the final image, and you don't want

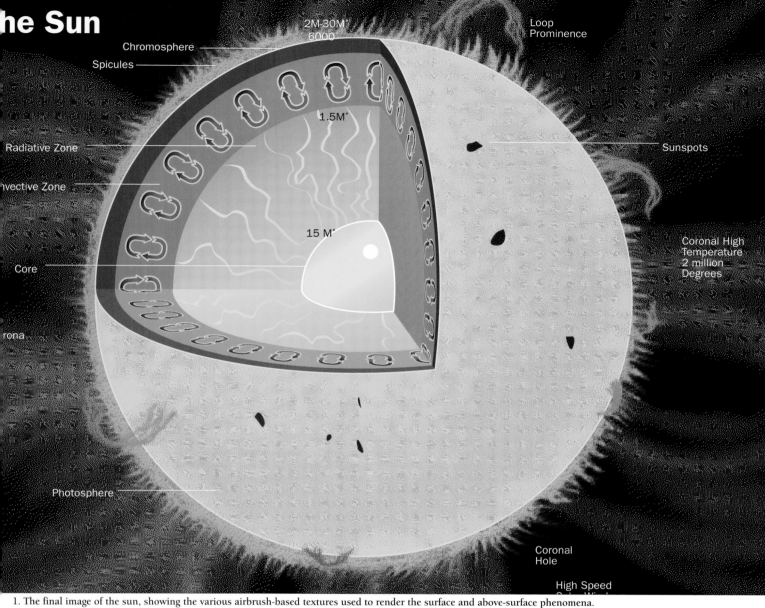

Loop
Prominence

2M-30M°
6000

Chromosphere

Spicules

1.5M°

Radiative Zone

Sunspots

vective Zone

15 M°

Core

Coronal High
Temperature
2 million
Degrees

rona

Photosphere

Coronal
Hole

High Speed

1. The final image of the sun, showing the various airbrush-based textures used to render the surface and above-surface phenomena.

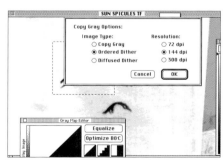

5. Scanner settings in place to produce a dither.

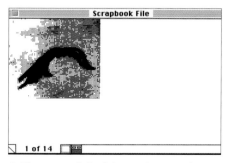

6. After I created the dither, I put it into the Scrapbook. From there I placed it into FreeHand.

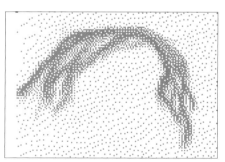

7. I placed the scanned image into FreeHand by selecting and copying the image, and then colored it.

electronic blends to overlap screened scans, or vice-versa. The two don't mesh well.

So I airbrushed the purple sprays and scanned them into TIFF's, using ThunderWorks software. (I had ruled out importing the art as PICT images, because PICT's, being line art, won't overprint, and thus wouldn't be transparent against the black background.)

ThunderWorks first converts an image into a half-tone, which you can use directly or further convert into other types of screens, such as "dithers."

Whereas a halftone employs a regular dot pattern, a dither is a different way of modulating tonality: it uses a mathematically-generated pattern of dots to simulate random-

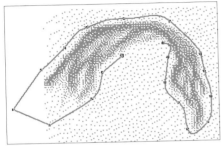

8. The area of the dither representing the loop prominence is segmented from the background by drawing a "clipping path" around it.

9. Then I pasted the cut-out loop prominence into the illustration as a high foreground layer.

10. In order to enter the type "Loop Prominence," I selected the type tool, clicked at the position where I wanted the type to go, typed the words, and then clicked "OK" to insert "Loop Prominence" into the illustration.

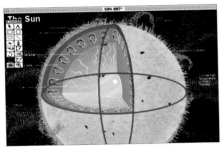

11. I used the circle and sizing tools to produce two ellipses, and aligned them at right angles to each other.

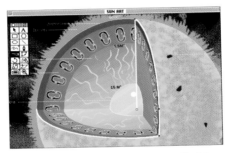

12. I used the cutting tool to remove all of the ellipses except the parts that defined the edges of the cutaway. I left these as thinner lines.

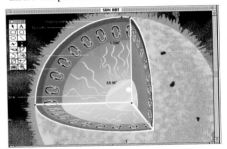

13. After drawing the construction lines from the corners of the cutaway to the center of the core, I had the three interior "slices" defined. I removed the construction lines, then did the shadings and blends needed to create the highlights and shadows, and the illusion of depth.

ness (2, 3, 10). In printing several irregular transparent textures which will overlap, dithers work better, because dithered colors mix together better than colors based on halftones, and there is less chance of moires occurring in the printing process.

Dithers are applied in layers in FreeHand, with the background layer laid down first, followed by the successive covering layers. For example, in figure 3, the background corona is Layer 10, the intermediate layer for the spicules is 41, and the surface of the sun is 50.

It may be helpful to follow the development of one of the imported textures from drawing board to

FreeHand. Figures 4 and 5 show the ThunderWorks settings for another piece of hand-drawn art, my pencil sketches to represent the sun's "loop prominences."

The duly dithered scan is placed in the Mac's "Scrapbook," a temporary storage area from which you can take something which you've scanned in—image, text, or type—and put it into an application program such as FreeHand (6).

I placed the scanned image into FreeHand by selecting and copying it (7). I also colorized it at this time. Then I drew a "clipping path" around the part of the dither representing the loop prominence, in order to segment it from the rest of

the background (8). I deliberately did not crop the image too tightly— I wanted some of the marginal dots to appear, so that they would give the impression of a fiery aura glowing off the edges of the prominence. After I cut out the prominence, I pasted it into the image (10).

CONSTRUCTING THE CUTAWAY

Rendering the cutaway view of the sun required the use of a number of techniques. The first order of business was to get the right angle "slices" for the projection. I drew two ellipses and enlarged them so that they appeared to be great circles on the sphere of the sun, set at 90 degrees to each other (11).

“I needed, among other things, to render four of the sun's fiery and turbulent surface phenomena. ”

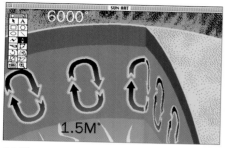

14. The arrow pairs on the right "plane" are actually made by cloning, rotating, and skewing the original arrow (eg., the one above "1.5M").

15. The original yellow arrow outline was drawn, then filled with bright yellow (100% yellow/40% red), and cloned to yield the bottom arrow, which was rotated into position.

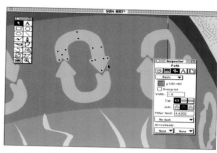

16. The color settings for the arrow outline.

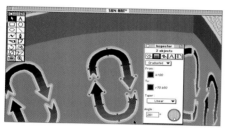

17. The inside of the arrow is given a graduated fill from black to purple.

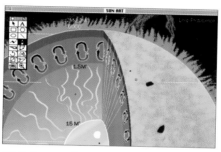

18. Before I could place the arrow pairs, I had to divide the three planes into apparently equal segments. Note the construction lines on the right face.

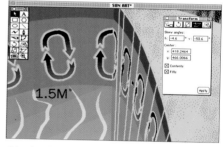

19. The skew settings for one of the arrow pairs.

20. Close-up of several of the skewed and rotated pairs of arrows. The construction lines were removed after the arrows were placed in their proper positions.

Then I ungrouped the ellipses, got the cutting tool and cut them where they intersected. This got rid of all the lines of the ellipses except the area that form the edges of the cutaway (12). From the three corners of the cutaway, I drew straight construction lines to meet at the visual center of the sun (13). This defined the three cross-sectional "planes" of the sun's interior; then I removed the construction lines.

To create the sun's core I used three smaller intersecting ellipses. The highlight spot and the bright midtones of the core were blended together with the blend tool.

The looping pairs of arrows representing the convection currents in the sun's convective zone (14) were all made from a single arrow (15) which was cloned, turned, rotated, and skewed to make the arrow pairs all appear to be on the planes of the cutaway (20). (In FreeHand terminology, the "rotating" and "skewing" tools are two of the four "Transformation" tools. The other two are the "reflecting" tool and the "scaling" tool.)

Before I could properly rotate and skew each arrow pair, and position it

in its proper place on one of the cutaway planes, I had to divide each of the three planes into apparently equal segments (18). Then, one by one, I duplicated the original arrow pair and rotated and skewed it into place (19, 20).

The Solar Darkroom

Pixels of Fire

In the discussion of the sun illustration on the preceding four pages, I discussed how I created the fiery phenomena on and above the surface of the sun: corona, loop prominences, spicules, and the surface itself.

In a nutshell, this was how the process worked: I either hand-drew or airbrushed a texture, scanned it, then imported it into FreeHand as a PICT image. The scanner converted my original image into a half-tone, which I then had it convert into a dither pattern, which mathematically scatters the dots to simulate a random array.

Once these dithered scans were opened in FreeHand, I colored them, then laid them down in overprinting layers—so that background layers would be visible through the transparent open spaces of the foreground layers.

This was a lot of work. I wish I'd had the Adobe Photoshop program when I did "The Sun"—I could have done all this in a fraction of the time, and not gotten into a dither.

Photoshop, from Adobe Systems, is a powerful image enhancement and manipulation program. It's primarily used, perhaps, to electronically retouch scanned photographs or other existing images.

CLIENT: NASA
TIME: 2 hours
SIZE: 2,250k
PROGRAM: Photoshop

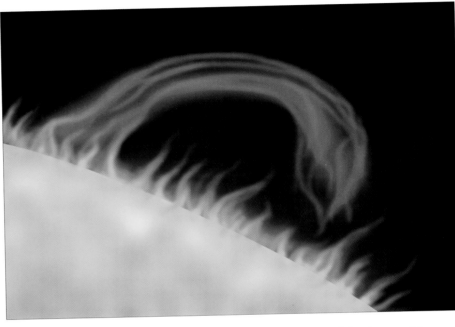

The program provides some very exciting features, including: a large set of digital filters that simulate traditional photographic features but go far beyond them in variety and flexibility; sophisticated color correction and creation palettes; and airbrush, pencil, and other painting and drawing tools.

As a postscript to our sun discussion, let's examine how we could render the features in Figure 9 of the original reconstruction, working entirely in Photoshop.

It's the airbrush feature that we'll be using here to re-create the sun's surface and above-surface phenomena in a completely different way than I described on the preceding four pages. We'll be electronically airbrushing these loop prominences and spicules directly onto the illustration, without having to bother

with scanning, dithering, making "clipping paths," and layering.

PIXEL-BASED PROGRAMS

Photoshop is what is called a "pixel-based" program. Pixels (short for "picture elements") are the grid of tiny display dots on a computer screen. Everything you see on a screen—images, type, lines, textures—are generated by applying tonalities to pixels. By contrast, in programs like FreeHand, which are called "object-oriented," the patterns which you instruct the program to apply to the pixels are produced by mathematically generated sets of vectors.

In pixel-based programs, everything you do—in our case, airbrushing sprays of different colors—is applied directly to this grid of pixels. Using the fine settings and controls Photoshop affords, we'll be able to

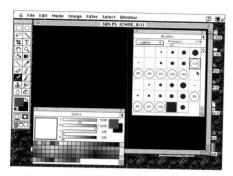

1. We open a new document in Photoshop. The airbrush pressure is set at a very light 11%.

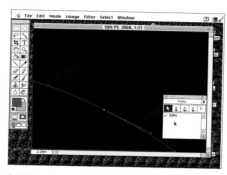

2. Using the pen tool we draw the segment of the sun's surface. It'll serve as a frisket.

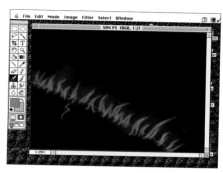

3. With a light airbrush pressure, we start lying down soft strokes . . .

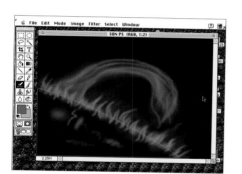

4. . . . to make the prominences and spicules.

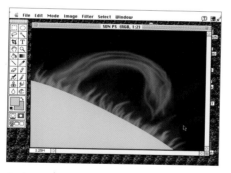

5. The outline of the sun is filled with yellow.

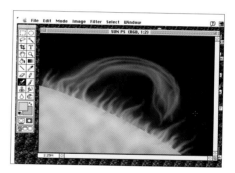

6. The finished image in Photoshop. Textures of hot glowing orange pixels have been sprayed onto the sun's surface.

render the soft, subtle effects you get with a "real" airbrush.

Let's start by opening a new document in Photoshop at 300 dots per inch. We go to the brush palette and select a large diameter airbrush—124 pixels—and take the color palette and adjust the sliders to produce the color we'll use for our first airbrush spray (1).

Also in this box, we set the application pressure at 11%. The higher the setting, the more electronic paint is applied to the pixels with each pass of the airbrush. Since we want to render soft, transparent sprays with black space visible

behind them, we choose a very low pressure setting.

Next we need to outline a portion of the sun's surface that will correspond to that shown in Figure 9 in the original reconstruction. The outline will serve as a frisket to which we'll later apply the sun's fiery surface colors.

We draw the outline with the pen tool (2), placing curve points just as we would in FreeHand or Illustrator, and the program smoothes them into a regular curve. The pen is a vector-based tool for drawing freeform lines and objects in order to create precise friskets and masks.

Now we can take our Wacom electronic stylus and tablet, which is serving as our airbrush and paper, and spray down our spicules and prominences (3, 4). When we're done we fill the outline of the sun's surface with a yellow color we've mixed in the color palette (5). The final step is to take the airbrush again and render the soft orange textures on the sun's surface (6).

This whole operation results in a much softer, continuous-tone look, which I find preferable to that created with the scans and dithers; and it's also a lot faster.

The Columns of the Parthenon

It's Only Fitting

National Geographic's Book Division was preparing *The Builders,* an encyclopedic book which would recount the principles and personalities behind the construction of some of the world's most famous structures: bridges, aqueducts, skyscrapers, tunnels, pyramids, cathedrals, and so on.

A set of striking photos would accompany the text of each chapter, and their purpose would be to show these man-made wonders in their most spectacular aspects.

One thing that the photographs couldn't show, at least for most of the older structures, was *how* the buildings were made, how the components were designed, and how they fit together.

In order to show how an older structure was built, illustrations were called for, and I was called on to do some of them. One of my illustrations would show how the Greeks built their columns by joining together, without mortar, a series of solid "drums."

The illustration had to be clean and it had to be simple—or as

CLIENT: National Geographic
TIME: 3.5 hours
SIZE: 300k
PROGRAM: FreeHand

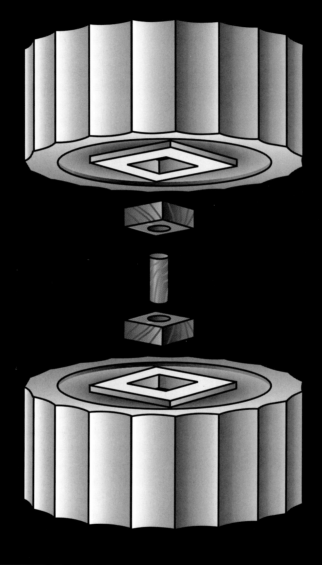

Dale Glasgow © National Geographic Society

simple as possible. A minimum of information was to be shown: just the column pieces and how they worked or fit together.

In general this selectivity is common to most scientific, technical, architectural, engineering, and cartographic diagrams. You want to figure

out how much detail can be left out, at the same time that you're deciding what to put in.

Things in the real world usually have a lot of individualizing aspects that get in the way of your perceiving their basic nature.

In the case of the columns, these aspects include discoloration, chinks and cracks from weathering, and various other results of decay or vandalism.

One of the illustrator's main tasks is to see through these superficial irregularities and show the structure of the object.

DEVELOPING THE ILLUSTRATION

There are a couple of interesting technical aspects of this illustration. The first involves the graphic rendering of a drum, and the 20 concave channels which the Greek master carvers chiseled into the outsides of the columns. The second is the matter of creating a mirror image of the drum.

The art director supplied me with a reference drawing of the construction of the column sections, which I used as a model (1). First I drew an ellipse to set the perspective for the column drum cross-section (2).

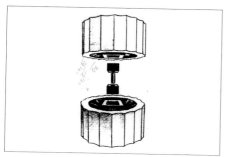

1. The client supplied me with this reference diagram, which I followed closely in my illustration.

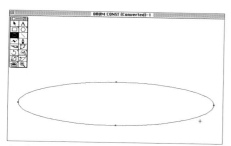

2. I kept the slanted perspectives of the reference drawing. To set the perspective for my cross-section, I drew an ellipse.

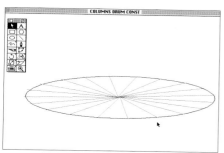

3. Then I divided the ellipse into 20 equal sections of 18 degrees each. Basically, I power-duplicated the first section 19 times.

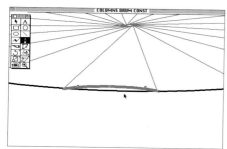

4. I drew a concave arc between the endpoints of one of the sections.

Then it was time to make a protractor. I divided the ellipse into 20 equal sections, which would correspond to the placement of the concave grooved channels.

To divide the ellipse I drew a line to its center, cloned the line, then rotated it 18 degrees to create the first slice. Then I power-duplicated this clone-and-rotation sequence 19 times (3). You'll notice that FreeHand rendered all the 18-degree sections on the plane of the ellipse.

The outer rim of each section then had to be given a concave arc that would form the top edge of one of the channels. I drew a slight curve with the FreeHand pen tool (4).

You don't need to click a whole lot of points to draw a curve in FreeHand. In this case only three points were required, the two endpoints and the midpoint.

I incised these concave arcs into the sections of one quadrant of the ellipse; then I used the FreeHand "reflect" tool to make a mirror image of this quadrant, which gave me the front 180 degrees of the ellipse.

Then I had to draw a quadrant of arcs on the rear of the ellipse (in perspective these are slightly flatter than the front arcs). I then reflected this rear quadrant, and the whole 360 degrees was done (5).

To create the cylindrical thickness of the drum, I used the knife tool to bisect the outline of the ellipse. I cloned the bottom segment and

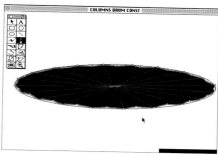

5. I filled a front quadrant of the ellipse with these arcs; then mirror-imaged that quadrant with the reflecting tool; then ditto the back.

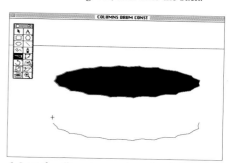

6. I cut the ellipse in two, then cloned the lower half and moved it down to form the base of the drum. The crosshair shows the position of the horizontal cut.

7. Two vertical lines are added to form the sides of the drum.

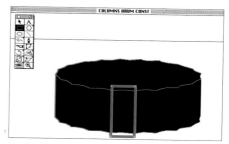

8. The first step in filling the outer channels with shadow-to-light graduations is to make rectangular fill blocks.

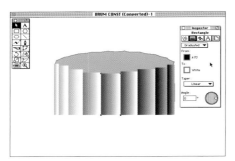

9. The example section gets a fill that graduates from 70% black at the left edge to white at the right edge.

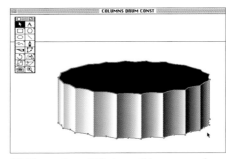

10. The graduated fills have all been cut-and-pasted inside the channel shapes.

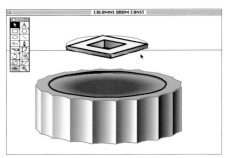

11. The square socket inside the drum is also given depth with graduated fills.

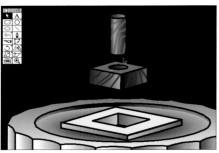

12. The "nut" and "dowel" which fit inside and align the drums to each other.

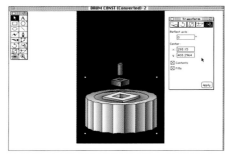

13. The objects to be reflected are selected, and the axis of reflection is set.

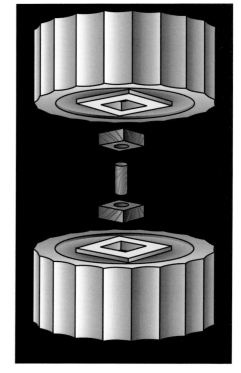

14. The reflected drum and parts. With the reflecting tool, the mirror image was generated in less than a minute.

pulled it down to form the base (6). The next step, after drawing the sides of the drum (7), is to fill the path for each concave channel with a graduated shadow-to-light texture, in order to render the smooth concavity of the channel. First you draw a rectangular shape whose sides are the sides of each channel, but extended at top and bottom for masking purposes (8).

This rectangle gets a fill that graduates from dark grey at left to white at right (9). The other channels are filled by cloning the fill block, then dragging the fill block over each channel shape, and cut-and-pasting the block inside the channel shape.

Then the graduation for each channel is adjusted, so that the channels have progressively more shadow from left (the light source) to right (10).

The surface of the drum was then drawn, with a recessed area in the middle. Into this recession was set a square socket. To get the right plane for the socket, I made a diamond shape to fit a scaled-down version of the initial ellipse (11).

Finally I drew the "nut" and "dowel" pieces which the Greeks fit into the square socket to firmly align the drums to each other (12)—but I still had to make the second drum.

FreeHand's reflecting tool makes a mirror image of an object by "reflecting" it across an invisible axis. The settings are shown in Figure 13, and the reflected top drum and its pieces are shown in Figure 14. (The dowel piece is not reflected since it is shared by the top and bottom drums.)

Gypsy Moth Defoliation

Fitting The Numbers To An Image

Backpacker magazine asked me to do an illustration showing the gypsy moth's total defoliation of acres as of 1992, by state.

This turned out to be a project in which there was no easy, obvious fit between the chart numbers and typography, and the image. It was a job in which showing the range of numbers posed special challenges.

Sometimes there's a basic goodness-of-fit. You find a symbol which you can get, to conform to a chart line or chart bars or pie chart slices. This was the case, for example, in "Drowning in Debt" and in "Humble Pie," both of which are discussed in this chapter (see pages 50–51 and 134–137).

At other times, you get numbers that are, well, a little weird, from the chartist's point of view. In the case of the gypsy moth there was an extremely wide disparity in the numbers (1). Virginia had 748,000 defoliated acres, Vermont only 83.

With this 9,000-fold difference between the high and low numbers, you'd almost need to plot them on a logarithmic scale to have any sort of meaningful *visual* relationship between 83 and 748,000. But that would be a totally distorted picture.

As an illustrator, one must resist any temptations to distort statistical

CLIENT: *Backpacker* **magazine**
TIME: 5 hours
SIZE: 450k
PROGRAM: FreeHand

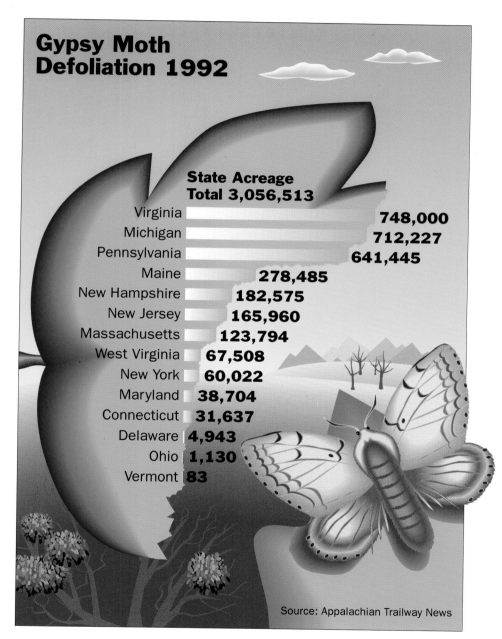

Gypsy Moth Defoliation 1992

State Acreage Total 3,056,513

State	Acreage
Virginia	748,000
Michigan	712,227
Pennsylvania	641,445
Maine	278,485
New Hampshire	182,575
New Jersey	165,960
Massachusetts	123,794
West Virginia	67,508
New York	60,022
Maryland	38,704
Connecticut	31,637
Delaware	4,943
Ohio	1,130
Vermont	83

Source: Appalachian Trailway News

relationships to make them easier to chart. You have to be careful not to use inappropriate scales; not to throw out high or low numbers; and not to make big differences appear small, or small differences big, by breaking scales. Whenever possible, your chart bars should start at zero.

DEVELOPING THE ILLUSTRATION

Enough of this statistical sermonette. In my charting of gypsy moth gluttony, not distorting the numbers meant that the bar chart plotting them would have a drastic taper from the high end (Virginia and

Michigan, both over 700,000) to Vermont's 83, which would barely be visible. I drew a quick rough plotting to see how drastic a bar-taper I would be facing (2).

Before precisely laying out the chart bars and typography, I wanted to come up with a conception of the image. This is good practice for bar charts, because (as I found out early on) you might take a goodly amount of time to lay out (say) vertical chart bars with slanting typography, but end up with an image that demands horizontal bars with right-reading typography, and you then have to lay it out all over again.

I knew that the two central elements of the image would be a gypsy moth, and some sort of foliage, perhaps a tree or leaf, and that behind them would be landscape in soft complementary colors. But the problem remained of coming up with an image in which the bars representing the numbers would naturally fit.

Several possible conceptions came to mind, and I jotted four thumbnails. The first idea was to put the moth and the numbers on two leaves, with vertical bars (3). This scheme didn't work—there wouldn't be enough room for the numbers and state names at the tops of the bars.

TOO MANY NUMBERS?

I might have suggested to the client that there were too many values—numbers and their labels—to chart clearly. An illustrator should

1. There was an almost 9,000-fold disparity between the high and low numbers I'd have to plot.

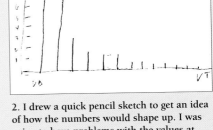

2. I drew a quick pencil sketch to get an idea of how the numbers would shape up. I was going to have problems with the values at the lower (right) end: not enough vertical separation among them.

3. The first conception was to put the moth and the numbers on two leaves. No dice. The vertical bars wouldn't have enough separation to allow the type to fit.

4. This isn't a drawing by my 2-year-old, but another thumbnail that was rejected. The conception lacked unity.

5. The most appropriate idea. This, too, would've required the numbers and state names to run vertically or diagonally, and so had to be rejected.

6. The last conception was the only one that would let the numbers and state names be right-reading. It was chosen.

always be aware of this option; nothing defeats the purpose of an information illustration more than a chart that's too cluttered for someone to read and comprehend.

You have to weigh the benefits of this course of action against the danger associated with it. Whenever you remove numbers from a distribution of statistics, you change the distribution. This often will distort the relationships among the numbers, which (again) should always be avoided. At any rate, I thought that as a professional chartist, I should be able to accommodate all 14 of the numerical values.

In my next idea, I put the moth on a leaf in the foreground, and the numbers on tree branches below it (4). This didn't work either. The conception didn't hang together. It lacked visual unity, and making the bars look like tree branches was too much of a stretch.

My next brainstorm was the most interesting conception: a moth eating a leaf. An image with two strong opposing elements. The bars would run vertically, each ending at a point where the moth has chomped off the edge of the leaf.

> **❝ Sometimes you get numbers that are a little weird, from a chartist's point of view. ❞**

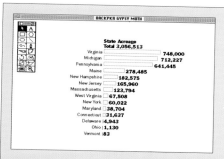

7. To produce the final rough, I first laid out the chart bars and the type.

8. Then I added the large outlines of the image. This rough was faxed to the client and accepted.

9. After filling in the moth and the leaf, I had a lot of negative space to deal with.

10. I added the background elements. The orange sky was chosen because it looked disturbing. FreeHand lets you try one color after another.

Unfortunately, this conception also had a fatal flaw: the numbers and state labels would have to run vertically or diagonally, and the thing would be almost impossible to read. (The type couldn't run horizontally because there wasn't enough difference in the numerical values at the lower end—the tops of the chart bars for Maryland, Ohio, and Vermont would have so little vertical separation that the characters wouldn't fit. Exasperation!)

Well, common sense finally made an appearance inside my forehead. It said, "Look, there's only one other solution. You have to turn the leaf on its side, so that the numbers and state names are right-reading at the end of horizontal bars." I drew the thumbnail for this idea, and it seemed to work (6).

ROUGHING IT AT THE MAC

At this point, I was ready to start work on the Mac. Before I started doing illustrations on the computer, I almost always went from thumbnails to a half-size rough, and then to a full-size, tight, final rough, before starting the final illustration.

But the computer makes it unnecessary to do these intermediate versions. Often, of course, a client requests successive roughs and you simply have to comply. Many times, though, the client gives you a go-ahead from a thumbnail or a

"rough-rough." If you have the image clear in your mind, you might as well go right to the computer. It's quicker and easier to draw, experiment, and make extensive changes at your screen. In this case, the final rough was actually a partly drawn final illustration.

The first step in rendering the final was the precise plotting of the chart bars, and the insertion of text (7). Then I drew the outlines of the primary shapes (8). This was the rough I faxed the client, who approved it.

I added the background elements, which would all be lighter or darker than the foreground (10). The orange sky was chosen for its menacing overtone. A great advantage of illustration software is that you can experiment with, and change, colors. It was quite painless trying out a bunch of different sky colors before arriving at the unobvious and wonderfully threatening orange.

Terminal Disorder

Mapping A Major Airport

An airport terminal is a simple, compact, easy-to-get-around place in which a few relaxed people stroll leisurely.

I wish. Of course, they're places where you have to understand and act upon a great deal of information, dash from one point to another to do it, and either have too little time—or way too much time, as we all know. The typical big airport, however good its flight operations, can be an info-nightmare for passengers and the friends or relatives they're meeting or leaving.

Since it really helps to know where things are in a terminal, a good, clear map can save you a lot of grief and wasted footwork. I was hired to do the terminal services map in the flight guide (1) to the Baltimore-Washington International Airport.

The existing map, an old paste-up job (2), had several major problems. First, it was a flat, two-dimensional diagram. Its heavy black lines, especially with its lack of shading or perspective, assaulted the eyes. It lacked zip. Second, the diagram was confusing or incorrect in key places (one of the main entrances was not even shown!)

Third, the typography was not properly set up, and was annoyingly inconsistent. Fourth, the symbols for some of the terminal services were

CLIENT: BWI Airport
TIME: 15 hours
SIZE: 425k
PROGRAM: FreeHand

unclear, and the symbols for the lower level were so reduced in size that they were almost unreadable without a magnifying glass. There was a lot of work to be done on this one. I sat down at the Mac.

DEVELOPING THE ILLUSTRATION

Along with the old map, the client sent detailed schematics of the terminal's upper and lower levels (3). I wasn't comfortable about beginning with just this paper information in

hand, so I showered and shaved and made a trip to BWI (about 65 miles). I cased the joint and took pictures. (Figure 4 shows one of the photos, a panorama I shot from outside the main gate.)

Not only was I trying to get a good feel for the place, so that I could do an accurate illustration; I also wanted to confront this airport for the first time and imagine the problems an airline passenger might have in trying to find his way around. I call

> **" It saves a lot of time to keep trees, cars, people, or other objects in your personal archive files. ""**

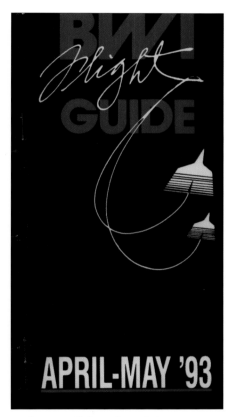

1. The airport flight guide needed a new terminal services map.

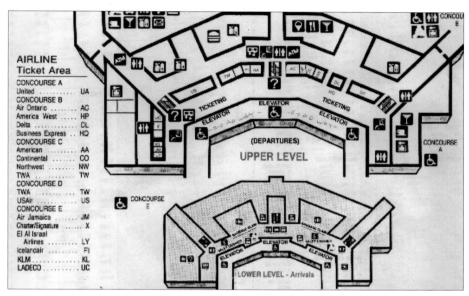

2. The old map was confusing, flat, incorrect, inconsistent, and hard to look at.

this activity "experiencing the information," and I think you need to do it in person in order to properly execute large-scale spatial diagrams.

This visit reinforced my plan to do the map in an isometric or "fake" perspective, from a point of view above and at an oblique angle to the upper and lower levels of the terminal. Even if no other changes were made to the old map, this pseudo-3D orientation of the planes of the two levels would add a little visual interest, which it certainly needed.

In my first thumbnail, I sketched the two planes in isometric perspective (5). My original idea was to have the upper terminal level overlap the lower level.

A series of three roughs followed. In the first (6), the two levels are rotated to about a 60 degree angle in isometric projection. Two small call-

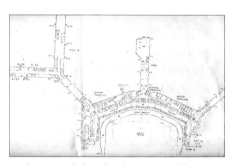

3. The original plans for the upper and lower levels. I used these as the basis for the small callout rendering of the complete terminal.

out-like sketches of the full terminal are at the bottom, one of them arcing out to the lower level.

I felt something was missing here:

4. A photographic montage I took outside the terminal.

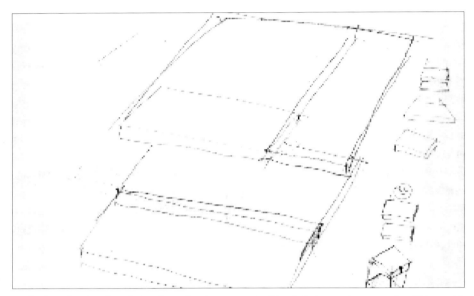

5. The first thumbnail, with the planes for the two terminal levels in isometric perspective. This would give the conception a 3-D look.

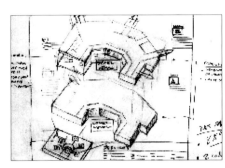

6. The first of three roughs, using the isometric projection. The two levels needed anchoring.

9. After drawing the two terminal levels on the Mac, I superimposed a system of grids for constraining and lining up the type blocks.

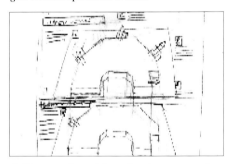

7. The second rough has a head-on perspective. The art director felt that this was too much like the old map.

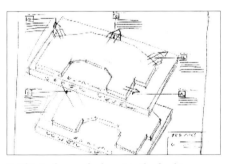

8. This is the rough closest to the final image. The solid planes now underlie the two levels. The overlapping of the levels was later canned.

an anchor for the two levels, which would also clearly separate them. For the second full-scale rough, I added the anchoring planes underlying the upper and lower levels (7).

The second rough (7) is similar to the old terminal map (2) in that its perspective is head-on. I preferred the head-on aspect because it corresponded to the view that the map reader would have as he faced the terminal. But the art director didn't like it, perhaps feeling that this con-

ception was too reminiscent of the boring old map.

The third rough (8) is the closest thing to the final rendition. The viewpoint of the isometric projection, and the solid planes underlying the two levels, both stayed. The overlapping of the two levels was canned, but otherwise the art director liked this conception.

In this matter of submitting alternative pencil thumbnails and "rough

roughs," the computer illustrator is in pretty much the same situation as his drawing board counterpart. The difference is in the tight final roughs, where the electronic illustrator often has a leg up. After the art director accepted the rough shown in Figure 8, I could go to the Mac and do the next, and final, rough on the computer. If it flew without the client requesting major corrections, I'd be able to use this illustration as the basis for the final, instead of starting from scratch again.

GRIDS AND SERVICES

In order to tightly render the final rough, and then execute the final image, I had to lay out a system of grid lines (9). I used these to center the title bar at the top, and to align

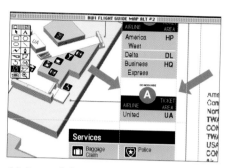

10. I wanted the concourse info blocks to line up flush with each other and also with the right column of the services menu below them. The alignment is assured by setting up grid lines, a very quick operation in FreeHand.

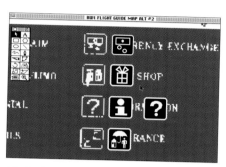

11. On the left are 4 of the icons in the services menu that needed work. Using 400% and 800% magnification, I could re-do them with precision.

12. The final. Some of the things I'd been working on are on the pasteboard, the work areas at the right and left of the illustration proper.

the concourse directories ("A," "B," etc.) and the services menu at the bottom right (10). The boxes containing the typography are given similar shapes and shading patterns, which makes it easier on the eye than the old map did.

After setting up the shaded boxes for the typography, and entering the type, it was time to confront the little icons in the services menu. Most were usable, but some were really confusing or needed cleaning up.

Figure 11 shows, in the left column, the original symbols for "Currency Exchange," "Gift Shop," "Information," and "Insurance." My revisions are in the right column, including alternative symbols for "Information" (the "i" was chosen).

Drowning In Debt

Uncle Sam Foots the Bill While Dale Glasgow Toes the Line

When I illustrate a statistical chart, or anything else for that matter, I keep one guiding principle in mind: the information is the most important thing. The illustration must engage the reader's interest, but always in a way that gives center stage to the star of the show: the information.

Nowhere is this principle more compelling than in a line, or "fever" chart, illustration. (A "fever" chart is so-named because it resembles the graph that plots a hospital patient's temperature.)

Whittle Communications hired me to do a line chart illustration for their quarterly business periodical, *Best of Business*. The chart line would plot the federal deficit from 1960 through 1988.

The client supplied the title, "Drowning in Debt," and sent a rough sketch of an idea they had, in which "IOU" in large letters appeared behind the underwater, descending chart line (1).

This conception didn't quite seem to hang together. What was needed, I thought, was a symbol of something being pulled down into the deep, but a symbol that could employ the chart line without (a) camouflaging it, or (b) distorting it. The position of the line at each even-year "node" had to be in the

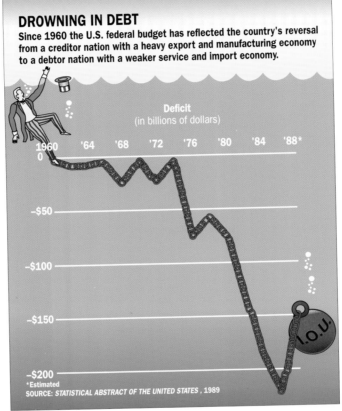

DROWNING IN DEBT

Since 1960 the U.S. federal budget has reflected the country's reversal from a creditor nation with a heavy export and manufacturing economy to a debtor nation with a weaker service and import economy.

Deficit
(in billions of dollars)

1960 '64 '68 '72 '76 '80 '84 '88*
0
–$50
–$100
–$150
–$200
*Estimated
SOURCE: *STATISTICAL ABSTRACT OF THE UNITED STATES* , 1989

right place along the vertical axis, indicating the dollar amount of the budget deficit.

I came up with two conceptions, one using a sinking ship as the symbol, the other a man (Uncle Sam) with a ball and chain around his ankle, pulling him underwater (2).

The client and I both liked the latter idea. I laid out the typography and the basic image, with a temporary chart line (Figure 3).

Separately I plotted the precise chart line and sent it to Whittle. Reflecting their concern with accuracy, they asked me to double-check

my positioning of several of the numbers (4). Fortunately, they were all right on the mark.

The key element in the illustration is the chain. I started by drawing the first chain link, leaving a small opening in it (5).

I cloned the link and moved the clone so that its left side was on top of the right side of the first link. But it appears to go *under* and through the bottom right curve of the first link (6).

The illusion works because the cloned link has an opening right at the place where it needs to "go under" the first link, allowing the first link to be "on top" at that intersection.

By duplicating successive links, I extended the chain, being exceedingly careful to follow the chart line. A section of the chain, superimposed on the chart line (which was later dropped out onto a background layer so that it wouldn't print), is shown in Figure 8.

Where the chart line made a jag, showing a change in the direction of the deficit, I rotated the next link to get the proper angle (7).

The final image is shown at left. I didn't count the number of links in

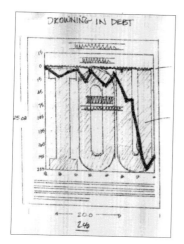

1. The client supplied this preliminary sketch.

2. I came up with two thumbnail conceptions more symbolically related to drowning.

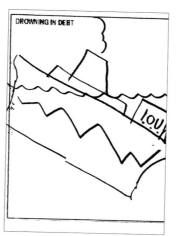

3. The basic image and typography are laid out.

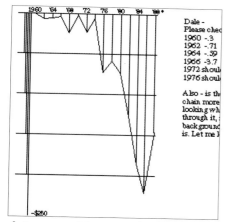

4. I constructed the precise chart line and verified the positions of the numbers for the client.

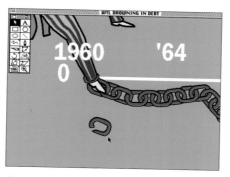

5. An opening is left in the first chain link.

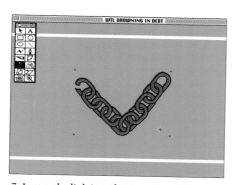

6. The cloned link has an opening, making it appear to "go under" the bottom right curve of the first link.

the chain, but I estimate that creating the whole chain took perhaps 20-25 minutes in FreeHand.

Creating them by hand would have taken at least 2 hours. One more example of how the capabilities of good illustration software saves a lot of time and drudgery.

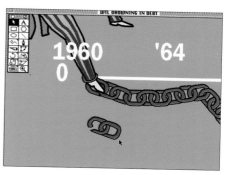

7. I rotated a link in order to create a change in angle.

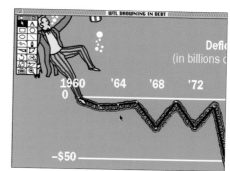

8. The chain follows the chart line very tightly.

CLIENT: Whittle Communications	SIZE: 110k
TIME: 5 hours	PROGRAM: FreeHand

Bird On A Wire

Draw That Tune

The *Training and Development Journal* was putting together an article on a subject that is, well, no fun: employee performance reviews. The problem with these dreaded rituals is that the ones being evaluated don't view them the same way as those doing the evaluating. (One nice thing about working for yourself is that you don't have such things to worry about.)

The art director gave me the controlling motif for the illustration: birds, some singing in harmony, others in cacaphony.

It was going to be one of those projects that I especially like and don't get nearly often enough: a conceptual illustration conveying dramatic, even conflicting, relationships among the "info-players" on the image stage.

Illustrations of this sort, if conceived and executed well, implicitly ask readers to do a bit of interpretation—the symbolism isn't as obvious as in a statistical chart, for example—and many people seem to be flattered by the demand. Maybe on a subconscious level it helps create rapport between author and reader.

DEVELOPING THE ILLUSTRATION

I decided to use the old line and wash style for this illustration. Although it isn't my usual style, here it seemed appropriate: it was important that each bird be distinctively outlined. The sharp outlines would symbolize individuality—it wouldn't

1. After the client gave me the birds theme, I submitted these roughs, which were approved.

2. Close-up of the hawk as scanned and placed into FreeHand.

3. Tracing over the scanned image in FreeHand eliminates the need to transfer an image to a drawing board.

4. After I drew the feather patterns and cloned them, I filled the upper part of the wing with them.

5. The color bar is a series of graduated fills, constructed of a progression of colors which have been "ramped" against each other.

6. To put the colors inside the curliques, you position the lines ("clipping paths") over the background (the colors).

7. The cut command or copy command is used to cut out the pieces.

8. The colors are pasted inside the curliques.

be a picture of just a bunch of birds on a wire; it would be a panorama of personalities (birdonalities?) singing their own tunes.

Using as models some illustrations in an old picture book, I drew a couple of pretty tight pencil roughs, which the art director accepted (1). These sketches were scanned and placed into Aldus FreeHand as TIFF files (2), and I started tracing over them with the pen tool to get strong lines (3 and 4).

By scanning images into FreeHand, you get a lot tighter a lot quicker. You don't have to transfer an image to a drawing board. You don't have as many generations to make of the same image. You don't have to redraw your lines all over again.

What you have is an electronic interactive sketch on the computer screen, which you can experiment with and change at will, and "undo" changes that you don't go for. You save time and become adventurous.

RAINBOWS AND CURLIQUES

As I mused about how to render the tunes of the birds on the right side of the picture, rainbows came to mind. A rainbow is a grand chord of color. If anything visually conveys harmony, a rainbow does.

I decided to use rainbow curliques to represent the notes, both to symbolize harmony and also to liven things up (look at what the little Apple logo does for the Macintosh console). I didn't want a bunch of boring birds on a wire.

With ramped graduated fills I created the color bar (5). After I drew

> **" I decided to use rainbow curliques to represent the notes, both to symbolize harmony and also to liven things up. "**

CLIENT: *ASTD Journal*
TIME: 12 hours
SIZE: 450k
PROGRAM: FreeHand

the lines of the curliques, I positioned them over the color bar (6).

In FreeHand terms, the color bar is the background, and the curliques are "clipping paths." After a clipping path is positioned over the background, you use the cut or copy command to cookie-cutter a piece of background and get rid of the rest of it (7). Then you hit the "paste inside" command to place it precisely inside the curlique (8). You might think of this as electronic masking.

The wire the birds are sitting on (9) was simply constructed. The endpoints and a few intermediate points (it could even have been one) were placed with the pen tool, and FreeHand generated the curved line.

9. The final illustration.

Canadian Cartographic Chit-Chat

A Big Country and a Lot of Information

In 1991 I did the third in a series of 18" by 24" poster maps of the top 20 U.S. housing markets for *Builder* magazine. Colliers Pierremont Inc., a Canadian real estate company, saw the illustration (1) and asked me to do a similar poster map for Canada.

This was the sort of project that makes many demands on your abilities to communicate visually. It would be a graphic filled with a great deal of information—information of several kinds.

First, there would be a map of Canada, rendered three-dimensionally. Onto this map would be plotted three distinct bar charts, respectively showing the new supply and the absorption of housing, in square feet; and the vacancy rate in percent; for 7 major Canadian cities.

The chart bars would need to be represented by three distinct shapes. In addition, there would be a table showing investment yields for various types of real estate. And finally, definitions of a couple of the measurements would have to be put in, clearly but unobtrusively.

Oh, well, I thought, it's a lot of stuff, but not enough to be overwhelming. Wrong. After I submitted the final illustration, I was informed by the art director that a second version, in French, would have to be

prepared, of course. Whew! Take my advice: always spell out what it is you're hired to do.

DEVELOPING THE ILLUSTRATION

The client supplied four types of information for each urban area (2). We decided that three of the measures could be shown comfortably, and decided to omit the inventory data. I did a very crude thumbnail to lay out the basic elements of the illustration (3).

From this I jumped to the first rough (4). Since I had the *Builder* illustration at hand, and in mind, I was able to sketch this out quickly. The client gave me the go-ahead.

The central image—the map with skyscrapers—was going to be a little static, I thought. A couple of helper images were needed to liven things up. On the first rough (4), I'd tried the ideas of a hurdler at the bottom left and a crane at bottom right. The client wanted to see other ideas.

A couple of them are shown in Figure 5. The client finally chose the man with the telescope, and the crane (see the Final image). The two subordinate images added some visual interest to perhaps the most boring parts of the entire illustration: the deadly dull definitions of housing absorption and net supply.

Next I turned to the chart bars. Having decided to use skyscrapers to represent them, I needed to draw them—or find them.

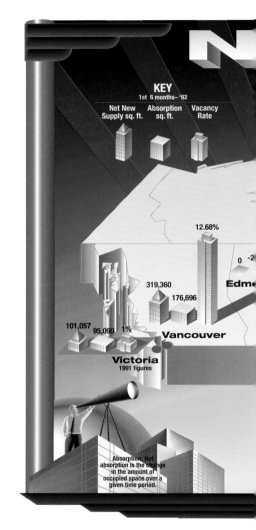

I knew I'd drawn skyscrapers before, and thought that I'd probably saved some of them to use in later illustrations. To find out, I went to my image storage files, or "swipe files," as I call them.

In a file called "Buildings FH3" (7), I store a bunch of images of all sorts of buildings, including some skyscrapers that looked like good candidates for chart bars (8). I placed three of them in the illustration and, using FreeHand's cloning

CLIENT: *Colliers Pierremont*
TIME: 23.50 hours
SIZE: 1,500k
PROGRAM: FreeHand

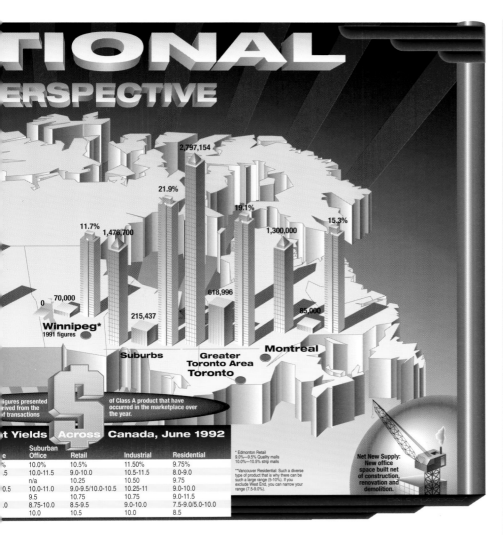

1. This is the original illustration I did of the U.S. housing market. It was an 18" by 24" poster.

2. The client supplied the housing data for each city. We used 3 of the measures, and left out the inventory data.

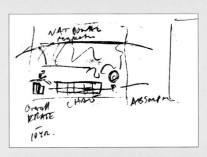

3. Most of my thumbnails are crude. Some are extremely crude. As long as they give you an overall *gestalt* for your graphic, it doesn't really matter.

Continued on the next page

and duplicating commands, I extended them to whatever height was required to portray the data values for each city. This is a very fast operation, and eliminates the need to custom-draw each building.

DRAWING THE MAP

To get the outline of the map, I scanned and traced the outline of Canada from a U.S. Geological Survey world map in the format of the Robinson Projection (9). (Incidentally, you can buy standard cartographic references like the Robinson Projection in electronic format, which you can load into your system and use.)

I traced over the scan with the pen tool, to quickly get it into the FreeHand environment. It then was time to add three-dimensionality.

After I put in the province boundaries (using a map from a geographic reference book as a visual model), I drew in the contour "cliffs" along the boundary lines. These were composed of a lot of individual rectangles, to which I added highlights and shadows with graduated fills in Aldus FreeHand (10).

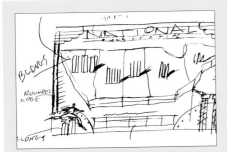

4. The first "rough-rough." I could see there were going to be a lot of chart bars posing as skyscrapers, but I knew I'd be able to move them around, to get as much visual separation as possible.

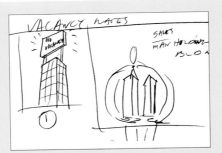

5. I tried to think of ideas for subordinate images for the corners—images that would add interest by suggesting real-world activity. These two were rejected.

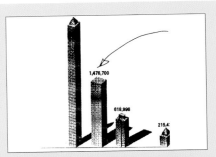

6. These are the skyscraper forms. Using FreeHand's cloning and duplicating commands, I adjusted their heights as needed to correspond to the numerical values.

7. My personal image files—"swipe files"—are grouped by keyword ("Birds," "Books," "Buildings," etc.), and alphabetically organized into folders ("FreeHand A-F").

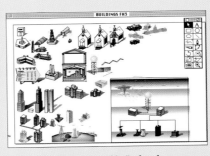

8. My building "swipe file." The skyscrapers I borrowed are in the bottom left corner.

9. For the outline of Canada, I scanned in, then traced, the outline in a U.S. Geological Survey world map in the Robinson Projection.

> **The two subordinate images added some visual interest to the most boring parts of the entire illustration: the deadly dull definitions of housing absorption and net new supply.**

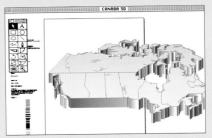

10. The three-dimensionality was achieved by making the map a slab. The "cliffsides" along the boundaries were created with FreeHand's rectangle tool, and shaded with graduated fills.

Lights, Camera, Action!

Creating a Cylindrical Pie With An Electrifying 3-D Drawing Program

Every once in awhile a program comes out which offers designers greatly increased capabilities, or which saves them a lot of time.

Infini-D, the extraordinary 3-D modeling program from Specular International, does both. It lets you create realistic graphic models of three-dimensional objects; give them color, surface textures, and lighting; and even animate them.

As soon as I got my hands on the program, I wanted to do an illustration, and of course the possibilities were infinite. After making a surreal bowling pin and a nifty screw, I decided to construct a cylindrical pie with a slice partially slid out (1). I'd done a great many pie charts, of

> **❝ I wanted something that looked real and had reflective surfaces, something that would resemble nothing in my memory. ❞**

course, but none with three-dimensional shape. I wanted something that looked real and had reflective surfaces, something so unusual in shape that nothing in my memory or

CLIENT: Glasgow & Associates
TIME: 3 hours
SIZE: 1,200k
PROGRAM: Infini-D

my archives could provide a starting point. I wanted to start from scratch and do a photographic rendering of something for which there were no reference photographs.

In building an image in Infini-D, you basically start with basic objects like spheres and cylinders (called "generic primitives"), move them around in the Infini-D "world" (its drawing board that looks like three-dimensional space), give them surfaces, fix their light sources, and otherwise manipulate them. You can even animate your creations.

You can do all sorts of things. You can join two objects or take one apart. You can also squash and stretch an object: you resize it along one axis while the other two are held constant.

A lot of this work can be done in traditional illustration programs, but it is extremely laborious, everything has to be specified in advance; whereas in Infini-D, the program does most of the dirty work for you.

For example, assume you have drawn a complex object like a set of bowling pins and you want to give them some complicated highlights and shadows.

In a non-3-D program, you have to specify each highlight, midtone or shadow, and then blend them together, pin by pin.

But in Infini-D, you merely set your light sources and camera angles, click the appropriate action, and the program does all the lights and shadows for all the pins, with one keystroke.

Let's look at how I constructed a simple 3-D object in Infini-D.

DEVELOPING THE ILLUSTRATION

I start by drawing the cross section of the slice (1), then the cross section of the rest of the pie (2), in separate files. These were drawn in Aldus FreeHand, an illustration program in which it's easier to draw basic shapes like these. You can make them in Infini-D, but it's quicker to use FreeHand's ellipse tool to make the circle and the line tool to make the slice lines. Later, if you decide to change, for example, the size of the slice, FreeHand will automatically communicate the changes to your Infini-D file.

FreeHand is able to do this because I export the two illustration files as "editions," which is the format Infini-D looks for when it imports documents from other programs (3). Then they're opened in Infini-D in its black drawing area, the "world" (4).

The operation, complex and mathematical and invisible to the illustrator, by which Infini-D creates a 3-D object out of a 2-D outline is called "extrusion." Figure 5 shows the big pie slice extruded into a cylinder. The smaller slice is also extruded and placed in the wedge cut out of the larger pie (6).

Then I create a color for a ball that will rest on each of the two cylindrical slices. This is done in a "surface information" dialog box which, in addition to specifying color, allows you to create the light, transparency, and reflectivity parameters for your object (7).

POINTS OF VIEW AND SOURCES OF LIGHT

The balls are then positioned on top of the slice pieces (8). In order to center each ball on its base, I switch to the four-view window, which shows top, camera, front, and right views, respectively (9).

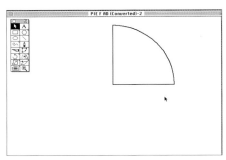

1. To create the 3-D pie chart, It was important to have slices that could be charted and then changed in a program like Freehand.

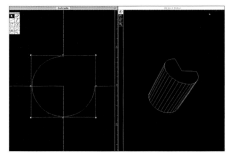

3. The parts of the pies were exported as editions so Infini-D could find them.

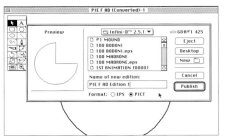

5. The beauty of a 3-D program is its speed. Here I add depth to the pie slice by extruding it in the extrude workshop of Infini-D.

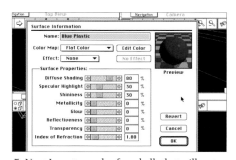

7. Next I create a color for a ball that will rest on each of the 2 pie slices.

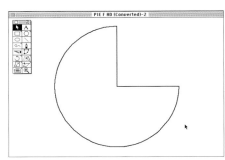

2. The second part of the 3-D pie chart was created in a second file.

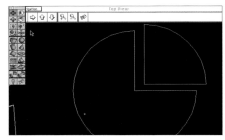

4. In Infini-D, the editions from Freehand are opened.

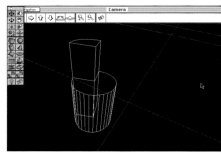

6. The smaller pie slice is given depth and positioned next to the larger pie, and the camera is positioned at the most aesthetic angle.

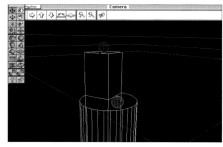

8. I then position the balls on top of the pie slices.

An object can be adjusted in one view or all views, and as an adjustment is made in one view, Infini-D automatically adjusts the position of the object in the others.

After the balls are positioned, I add an extra light source (10), then place a transparent surface between the lights and the objects, to soften the intensity of the light (11).

Next I move the camera around in order to get the best angles to optimize the shadows and accentuate the contrasts (12).

Then I do a "spot rendering" of the image. In a spot rendering, you select a portion of an object and Infini-D applies your colors, textures, and other surface qualities.

I select the ray trace tool, the best (but slowest) rendering mode, to check my lighting and shadows (13). Satisfied, I use the tool to render the entire final image (14).

AN ELECTRONIC LATHE

Infini-D also has another drawing environment called the Workshop. Here you can lathe objects, make custom extrusions, and create freeform objects.

This is the place to make complex 3-D models, and could be the subject of a lengthy demonstration (which is beyond the scope of this book).

Infini-D is but one of a fast-growing class of exciting 3-D modeling, rendering, and animation programs

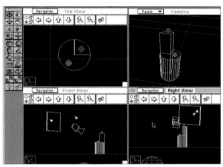

9. I switch to four views to get the balls positioned accurately on top of their base—if they are too high, they will cast a big shadow; too low, and they will be submerged in the pie slice.

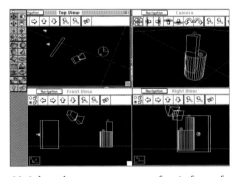

11. I then place a transparent surface in front of the lights to soften their intensity.

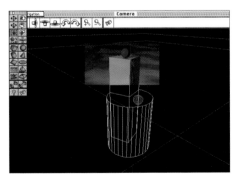

13. I spot render the image with the ray-trace tool (the best shading mode possible of four possible types) to check my lighting and shadows.

that will let you really expand your graphic horizons. Other first-rate programs in this group include Adobe Systems' Dimensions;

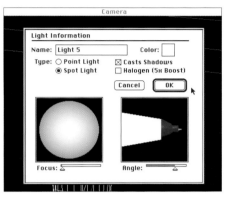

10. I added an extra light source to brighten my scene up.

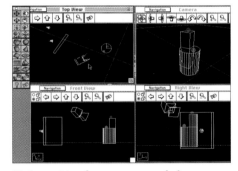

12. I reposition the camera to tweak the scene for shadows and contrast of surfaces.

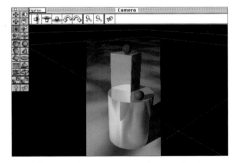

14. I then use the ray-trace tool to render the final scene. This file will be used as a TIFF file for printing in QuarkXPress.

MacroMedia's Macromind Director, Swivel 3D, and MacroModel; and Strata Inc.'s StrataVISION.

Dale's Bales

Cloning and Blending Bundles

An illustrator just getting started may have an "A-list" of fifty or sixty prominent periodicals with big national circulations that she'd like to draw for. Jobs for the other thousand or so magazines— those single-subject journals with much fewer than a million readers— would be taken on primarily to put food on the table.

Actually, I don't know any illustrator with such a pretentiously narrow bandwidth of interest. I've concocted this straw-person to make a point.

Whereas assignments with *U.S. News & World Report,* or *National Geographic,* are challenging and rewarding, so too are the projects you do for industry or trade magazines or professional journals.

In fact, some of the most interesting illustrations I draw are for single-subject publications. A magazine for farmers, *Farm Forum*, is an excellent case in point.

It might sound like a boring sort of periodical, cut-and-dried as a tobacco sheaf, but the staff puts together articles with a lot of interesting illustrations. In one that I did, the sizes of the bellies of growing pigs were portrayed graphically as a series of sports balls: marbles, golf balls, softballs, basketballs.

CLIENT: *Farm Forum* magazine
TIME: 5 hours
SIZE: 450k
PROGRAM: FreeHand

Use Your Time Wisely
Focus on activities that will give the greatest return on your time investment

In the present project, I was hired to do an illustration for an article on the problem of how farmers should prioritize their tasks in order to use their time more wisely. My job was to create a graphic for a sidebar which classified farmers' activities into four categories, which were ranked according to their urgency and importance.

The art director sent me a summary matrix of the four categories (1) along with the text of the sidebar, which was entitled, "Where does the time go?" Accompanying the text was a rough drawing (2), in which a tractor was pulling a hay wagon which carried something that looked like a chart.

At the top was a line that jagged up and down, like the line on a statistical line graph, or "fever chart." I liked the tractor-wagon idea, but a line chart wouldn't be appropriate for the information to be illustrated.

A fever chart— which someone named after the graph tracking a hospital patient's temperature—plots changes in quantities over time. This is a statistical relationship.

My information, however, was not numerical; it was topical. The relationships among the categories were those of similarity and difference, not quantity. The information in the categories would be compared and contrasted, not counted. A diagram resembling any kind of statistical chart—fever chart, bar chart, or pie chart—would be completely inappropriate.

It is exceedingly important as an illustrator to keep in mind that most clients are not statisticians or chartmakers, and it's up to you to choose the appropriate type of graphic vehicle for the kind of information you have to illustrate.

> ❝Some of the most interesting illustrations I draw are for single-subject publications.❞

I did a couple of quick thumbnails (3). The one on the left had that "charty" look and was immediately discarded. I decided to use the other conception, which would translate into four stacks of hay bales, the stacks having different heights, and corresponding to the four categories mentioned above.

DEVELOPING THE ILLUSTRATION

With the image in mind—it was a simple conception—I opened a new illustration in FreeHand. The first thing I had to do was find a tractor. I knew I'd done an earlier illustration for the magazine, a chart tracking corn and soybean prices, in which I'd put a tractor and wagon (4).

I went to the file containing that illustration and clicked on the tractor-wagon to select them. I copied them and brought the copy into the new file (5). The deep gondola of this grain wagon didn't fit into my plans, though; I wanted a flat bed.

I ungrouped the gondola so that I could take it apart. I took the gondola off and put it aside, leaving the wheels and shadow in place (6). To construct the flat bed, I cut off the top part of the gondola and filled it with flat color, resulting in a simple 3-D rectangle for the flat bed (6).

This would also have been easy to do using FreeHand's rectangle and line tools; but cribbing from the gondola ensured that my wagon bed would have the same perspective angles as the gondola and tractor.

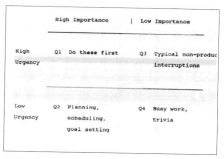

1. The basic information to be shown was this classification of farm activities into four ranked categories.

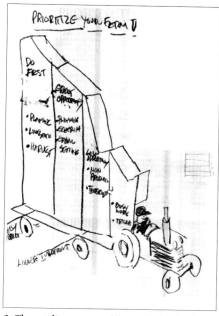

2. The art director sent this rough sketch of a tractor pulling a line chart on a wagon. The tractor/wagon idea worked but the chart didn't—the information wasn't numerical.

3. I chose the idea on the right—four stacks of hay bundles for the four activity categories. The perfectly regular difference in the stack heights would suggest ordinal, not quantitative, relationships.

Then I simply pulled the flat bed straight down to its position over the wheels. By taking the shape of the platform from the gondola of the earlier illustration, I ensured that the angles of perspective would all be the same.

Next I had to build the first hay bundle—from which all the others would be cloned. I went back to the old trusty grain gondola (5), and this time I cut off part of the bottom and used it as the basis for the shape (8). As with the flat bed, adapting the shape from an object in the earlier illustration gave this proto-bundle the proper angles, so that it would lie on the hay wagon in correct orientation to the front, back, and sides of the hay bed.

MAKING HAY

Now we have this "proto-bundle" of hay that looks like a brick. We've got to soften it up. We start by taking the pen tool and drawing rounder lines for the bale outline, using the "brick" as the reference shape so that we keep the relative dimensions and angles (9, 10).

Figure 11 shows the completed outline. Now we can put in the blends which will give the sides and end of the bale a softer, rounder look. Blending is one of FreeHand's key features for creating highlights, shadows, and the illusion of depth.

A blend creates a series of intermediate steps that produces smooth transitions between two elements, such as lines, shapes, colors, and

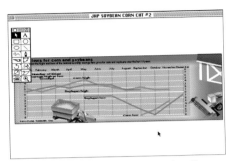

4. I borrowed the tractor from an earlier illustration for the same magazine.

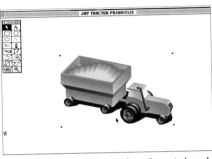

5. The tractor/wagon was selected, copied, and brought into the new illustration file.

6. I took the gondola apart by "ungrouping" it—removing the electronic blueprint FreeHand uses to hold together the points and lines of a graphic object.

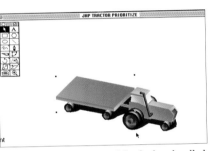

7. I selected the ungrouped flat bed and pulled it straight down to rest over the wheels.

8. I cut off part of the old gondola (5) and used it as the geometric basis for the first hay bundle.

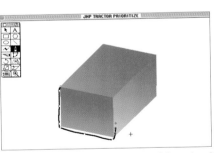

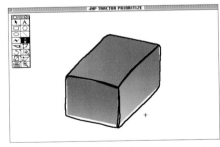

9, 10. We start rounding the lines of the cube, drawing curved corners and otherwise putting in natural irregularities with the pen tool.

fills. It's more mechanical to do on the computer than with an airbrush, of course, but the result is similar.

We begin preparing the elements to be blended by coloring the three visible sides: a light gold for the top, a dark gold for the side, and a medium gold for the front (12).

Then we clone the side and pull the clone up to overlap the top, creating a thin closed shape on the right edge (13). The blend command (13, 14) automatically puts in a smooth color transition, from dark gold to light gold (15).

The other sides are blended the same way. Then the construction lines—which we had to draw in order to define the objects to be blended (in FreeHand terminology, to make them "closed paths")—are removed. The twine is added as lines with a couple of fills (15).

After we size the hay bale to fit the flat bed, we place one bale at the front, then clone it three times and move the clones one back of another (16). We keep on cloning to build up the four stacks (19).

Now we can place the type on the ends of the bundles. In the text tool mode we type each text element, then place it in position. But it's out of kilter. Look at Figure 17: the type needs to be slanted to be in sync with the orientation of the bales and the vehicles.

We need to select the skew tool and vertically slant all the type ele-

ments, so that they have the same orientation as the bales and the vehicles (18).

Finally, we add a few more details, including the farmer looking with a baleful eye at all the prioritized activity categories on the ends of his hay bundles. Perhaps more importantly for the image, we put the variously colored cubes (representing the cat-

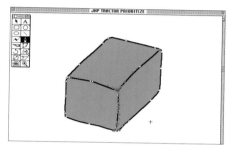

11. The completed bundle outline.

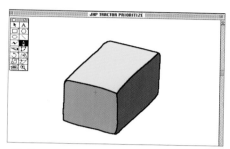

12. We put in the three colors to be blended.

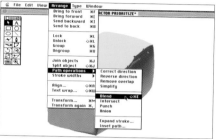

13. By slightly overlapping the top and side polygons, we produce a thin zone of intersection which will receive the color transition the blend command generates.

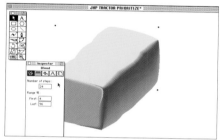

14. We choose the number of intermediate blending steps—in this case, 24.

15. The final bale. The lines for the pieces of tying twine have been cut with the knife tool at different places so that we can fill them with different shades.

16. We size the bale to fit the bed, then clone three more.

17. We start placing type that we've entered in using the text tool feature.

egory numbers) on top of the stacks to add some color interest and provide visual relief (19).

18. Since the text blocks appear in horizontal alignment, we skew them to slant them to the orientation of the bales and vehicles.

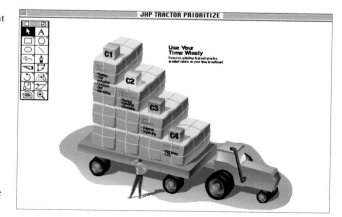

19. The final. We've put the variously colored cubes on top of the stacks to add some visual interest.

Wireless Network

Frequency-Hopping Your Blues Away

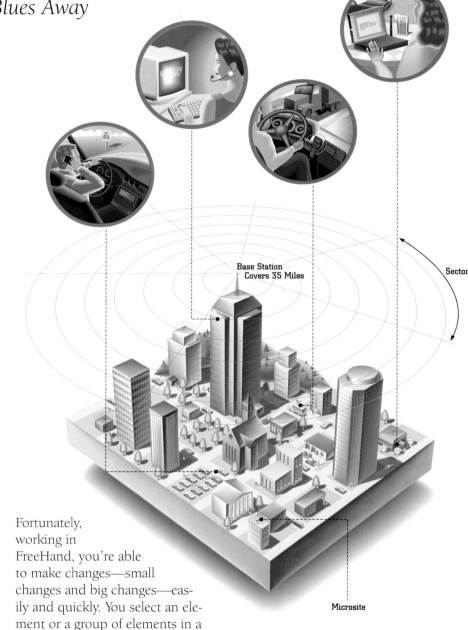

Base Station
Covers 35 Miles

Sector

Microsite

Geotek Industries, Inc., is developing a wireless communications network, GEONET ™, in major cities and metroplitan areas across the U.S.

The network, using frequency-hopping technology, covers areas of up to 35 miles radius with a single base station, and is accessible to subscribers who may either be in stationary sites like offices or homes, or in mobile locations like cars and delivery trucks.

For their annual report, GEOTEK needed an illustration of how the system works in a typical service area. The image would need to show both the placement of the base station and auxiliary stations ("microsites"), and also examples of various business users.

This would prove to be a very complicated illustration, with several interesting and difficult technical aspects. We'll touch on 3: the construction of perspective lines; building up a city block in perspective; and rendering concentric elliptical wireless waves.

As is the case with annual reports, this was no place for carelessness, imprecision, or anything less than showcase work.

Throughout the design process, the client asked for specific changes and suggested various improvements, all of which had to be implemented under extremely rigorous constraints with respect to size, position, line, color, and typography.

Fortunately, working in FreeHand, you're able to make changes—small changes and big changes—easily and quickly. You select an element or a group of elements in a picture and do whatever you want to with them—without changing or affecting other parts of the illustration. If you're not satisfied with your changes, just undo them and try other ideas. No problem.

Once you get used to this freedom and power, it's hard to go back to the old airbrush.

DEVELOPING THE ILLUSTRATION

The client supplied a thumbnail sketch of a city block, drawn in rough 3-point perspective, with 4 overhead close-ups, each of which was to show a different type of business subscriber to the system (1).

The first order of business was to construct the precise perspective line grids from the 3 vanishing points, to correspond to the "wide-angle-lens-shot" view of the block. First I drew a diagonally tilted square which would form the base of a city block (2).

Next I drew lines converging to the 3 vanishing points (3). I cloned one of these diagonal lines and moved it down slightly, creating an extremely narrow-angled 3-point ray (4), then power-duplicated this action a number of times (5 and 6) to create the first perspective grid.

In a similar fashion I created the other two perspective grids. Figure 7 shows the position of all 3 grids on a (greatly reduced) FreeHand illustration window.

With the perspective grids in hand, it was time to build the block. First I drew the "slab" of the block (8), then I laid out the street pattern with the cars and trucks on it (9). This formed the basic framework for the buildings and everything else in the scene.

Then I drew the basic outlines of the buildings (10).

To help in organizing the illustration—enabling me to work on one thing at a time while keeping everything else in position—I stored different design elements, such as buildings, and cars and trucks, on different layers in FreeHand.

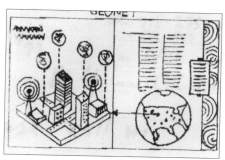
1. The client supplied the basic approach with this thumbnail.

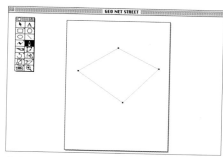
2. To provide a frame of reference for the perspective line grids, I drew a diagonally-tilted square, corresponding to the outline of the city block.

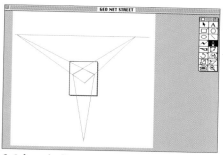
3. I drew the lines converging to the vanishing points.

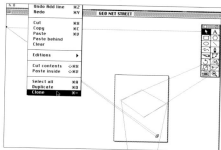
4. The first 3-point narrow-angled ray is created through cloning and moving one of the first lines.

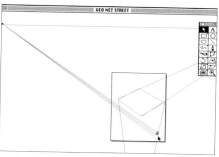
5. The ray is power-duplicated . . .

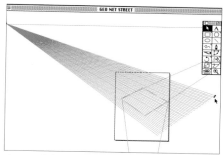
6. . . . And the result is the first grid.

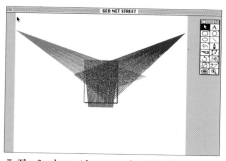
7. The 2 other grids are produced in the same way, by cloning and power-duplicating.

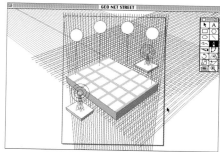
8. With the grids in place, I drew, in precise perspective, the "basic slab" of the city block.

Using layers, you can bring things up to the "current drawing layer" and put them back on lower layers, on a wonderfully carefree basis.

The final city block is shown in Figure 11. In developing the city, I had the perspective grid lines in the highest layer, which let me draw everything—buildings, windows, streets, vehicles, etc.—in precise perspective (12).

STUDY OF WOMAN WITH LAPTOP

There were four close-up images of hypothetical GEONET ™ users to be drawn and positioned above the skyscrapers (22). It may be useful to review quickly the evolution of one of them (the picture on the far right, a woman working at a laptop).

The first rendering was a sketch supplied by the client (13). This gave the basic situation, but obviously had to be brought to life. I did a rough, based on the sketch, which was marginally more interesting (14).

Discussing this with the client, I decided to give the laptopper a sex change, take her out of the dark, give her a view and a glass of lemonade, and put something to look at on her screen (15).

All this was needed, I thought, to make the little picture something more than a glorified icon, and give it depth and realism.

Constrained to fit the image into one of the four red circles, I simply cut and pasted it in, using the so-

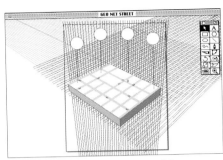

9. The street pattern is laid out and the cars and trucks plunked down.

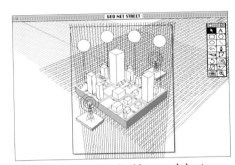

10. The outlines of the buildings and the 4 overhead close-ups are added.

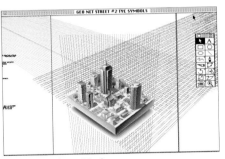

11. The final city block.

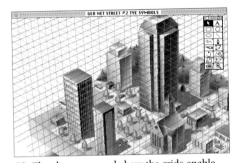

12. The close-up reveals how the grids enable you to draw everything in precise perspective.

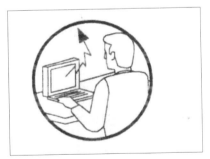

13. The client supplied the first rendering of the woman at the laptop.

14. She's still a he, but gradually taking on signs of life.

named commands ("cut" and "paste inside") in FreeHand (16).

DON'T BE WIRED— GET WIRELESS

The concentric ellipses emanating out from the tip of the highest skyscraper (the "base station") illustrate the network's coverage of a 35-mile-radius service area from a single

primary command center (22).

Constructing these elliptical "wireless waves" is a chore to do by hand, but a simple matter in FreeHand.

First you draw an ellipse to size, using the ellipse drawing tool (17). Then you clone this ellipse and reduce it, using the scaling tool, to

15. It was time to bring her into the real world. These elements added dimensionality and realism, essential if the image was to be anything but an icon-like object.

16. The image is cut and pasted into one of the four circles.

17. To draw the red concentric elliptical wireless waves, you first draw the largest ellipse.

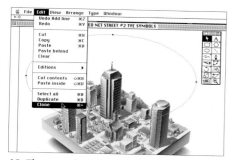

18. Then you clone it and reduce it to the size of the smallest ellipse you want.

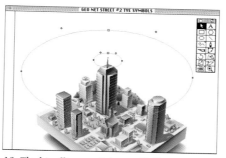

19. The big ellipse and the small ellipse are selected to be the outer and inner paths of a blend.

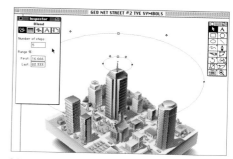

20. FreeHand is directed to do a 5-step blend.

21. The result is a set of 5 concentric ellipses, evenly graduated from the small to the largest ring.

the size of the smallest ellipse (18). Select the big ellipse and the little ellipse (19), and tell FreeHand to blend them in 5 steps (20) which generates the 5 intermediate ellipses which are evenly graduated in size from the smallest to the largest (21).

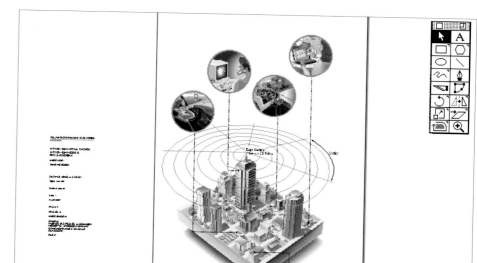

22. The final illustration.

CLIENT: Geotek Industries
TIME: 25 hours
SIZE: 2,300k
PROGRAM: FreeHand

FreeHand's Transformers

How to Clone, Slant, Stretch, Turn, Flip, and Change the Size of Objects

As you probably have realized by now, FreeHand's powerful drawing tools and features enable one to construct complex illustrations in far less time than it takes to do them by hand.

However, one of FreeHand's most endearing labor-saving capabilities comes into play not when you are doing an original drawing, but when you have to produce several versions of that drawing. The versions may either be identical to the original, or changed in some way(s).

With FreeHand, you don't have to redraw shapes to make more of them or to change them. You use its set of features called "transformation tools." They are the **rotating**, **reflecting**, **scaling**, and **skewing** tools, and they're used to best effect in combination with the **clone** and **duplicate** object-copying commands.

Although FreeHand is my primary drawing program, most state-of-the-art graphics programs (Adobe Illustrator, for example) have similar capabilities for transforming elements—and, for that matter, doing the other illustrating tasks we discuss in this chapter. Get FreeHand or Illustrator, or browse *MacUser* for the latest software reviews and comparisons, and you're headed in the right direction.

In many of the lessons in this chapter we discuss how certain effects are easily, quickly, and precisely obtained by using FreeHand's transforming tools.

Now let's be a little more systematic. Let's look at some examples of what these amazing tools can do to a simple shape, which we'll refer to as "the original."

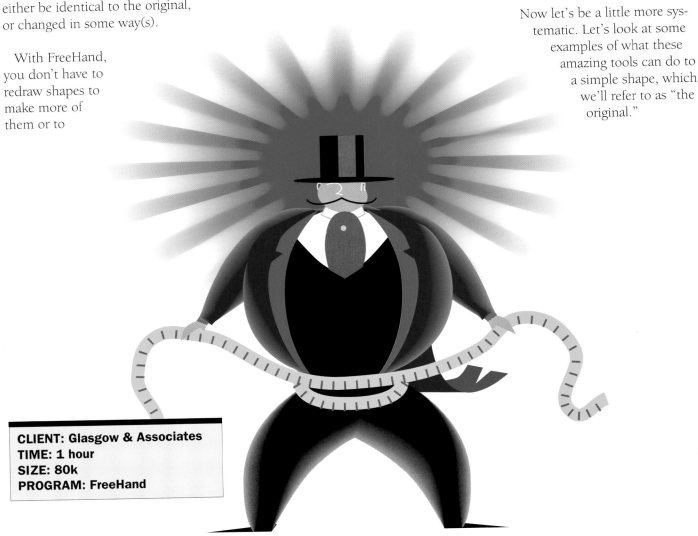

CLIENT: Glasgow & Associates
TIME: 1 hour
SIZE: 80k
PROGRAM: FreeHand

Our original shape is a small icon, a tycoon tightening a measuring tape around his ample abdomen (this guy was used in an illustration about corporate downsizing and belt-tightening):

Let's say that we need two of these symbols to use in a graphic. The simplest way to produce them is either to clone or duplicate the original image.

Cloning produces an identical copy directly under the original, which you can then pull out and position where you want it:

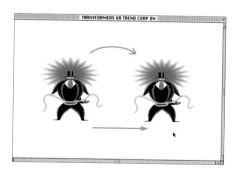

There was a film "Body Double." Was it about this guy?

Duplicating also produces an identical copy, but the copy is slightly offset from the original:

Here, too, you can pull the duplicate to wherever you want to position it.

TOOLING AROUND

Now that we have these two ways to copy an object, let's look at the four tools and see what effects we can generate with them.

Suppose that we want 5 identical copies of the original to surround a center object. This object will be a 5-pointed star.

After drawing the star, we position the tycoon symbol at the end of one of its arms:

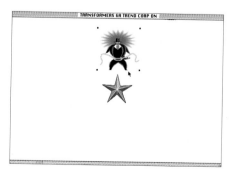

Now we clone the original and use the **rotating tool,**

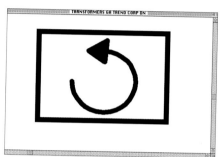

to turn the clone 72 degrees around a point at the center of the star. (FreeHand always transforms an object in relation to a fixed point, which can be anywhere you choose to place it.) This gets us:

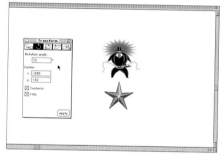

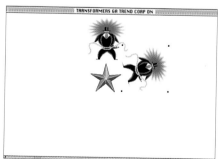

To produce the three remaining symbols, we don't have to do the two step clone-and-rotate sequence for each one. Rather, we **"power-duplicate"** this sequence three times and FreeHand generates three more clones and turns each one 72

more degrees around the center point, and places it in the image:

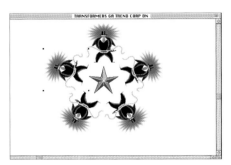

This is a simple illustration, certainly, but the tremendous timesaving power of cloning, rotating, and power-duplicating on a larger, more complex scale can easily be imagined. Try them, you'll like them.

What if we want to create a mirror image of the original? We use the **reflecting tool,**

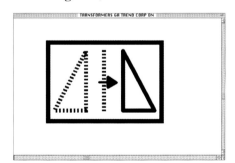

which makes a mirror image of an object by reflecting it across an invisible axis. Here is the dialog box :

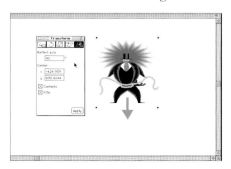

Here's the flopped image:

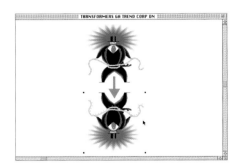

Or, we may wish to change the size of the original. Here we choose the **scaling tool,**

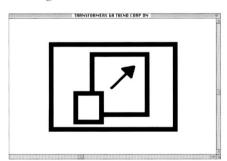

to reduce or enlarge an object or a group of objects:

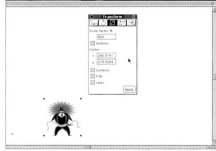

Does he have delusions of grandeur?

Finally, we might want to change the apparent plane that the object is resting on. Here we choose the **skewing tool,**

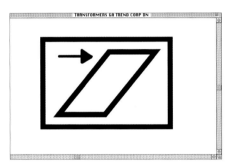

We can, for example, drag the element laterally to slant it horizontally:

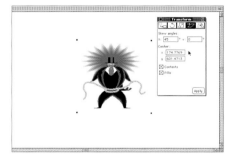

This poor captain of industry is really getting bent out of shape. He needs to think about taking early retirement.

Or we can drag the element up or down to stretch it vertically:

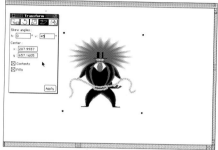

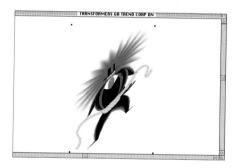

Or we can drag diagonally, which slants and stretches the object horizontally *and* vertically:

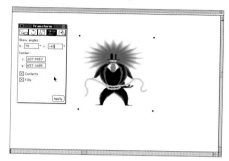

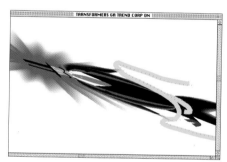

Now, don't you wish you could treat your boss like this?

It's perhaps uncomfortably obvious to a non-computer illustrator how much time and sweat these tools save. I won't dwell on it. All I'll say is, "Tired of spending hours of quality time drawing repetitive shapes? Get FreeHand, or Illustrator, or some other good illustration software, and see how satisfying time leverage can be."

Electronic Contour

States of the Arts

W hen your assignment is to show statistical information for a number of categories at a given point in time, you have several choices. The most common graphic vehicles are bar charts, pie charts, tables, and maps.

When you have fifty categories, it's difficult to design a bar chart or pie chart that's readable—the bars will be bunched or the slices will be slivers. Unless the categories are geographic. Then you can usually render them on a map.

Unless you have something like Kansas counties, the outlines of the geographic subdivisions will usually be irregular, so that they will not be a visual burden to the reader. Besides, most people like to look at maps (a theory of mine).

You can also put more than one measurement on each geographic unit of a map. That was important on the project we'll look at next.

Governing magazine asked me to draw a U.S. map comparing state funding for AIDS programs to that of the Federal government, on a relative basis (the art director sent the data shown in Figure 1).

There was a second set of data, which we'll call a "side element," which broke down the uses of State

CLIENT: *Governing* magazine
TIME: 15 hours
SIZE: 156k
PROGRAM: Dimensions, FreeHand

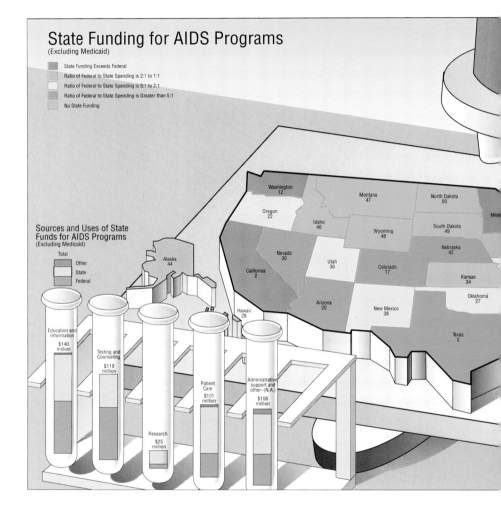

AIDS program funds; but these numbers were aggregate.

DEVELOPING THE ILLUSTRATION

Basically, I had to solve two conceptual problems. First, I needed to find an appropriate symbol or symbols to give the image a medical context. Second, I had to decide what to do about the side element.

Three thumbnails later (2), I decided to let the map be a specimen under a microscope—the thumbnail at the bottom. The side

element information would be contained in a rack of test tubes in the lower left.

This conception would have unity at the same time that it presented two independent data sets.

First off, I had to drum up a 50-state map. Sometimes I think I could draw one with my eyes closed, but fortunately, working in an electronic environment, I don't have to. I've drawn many maps and then saved copies of them, with type removed, in my archive files.

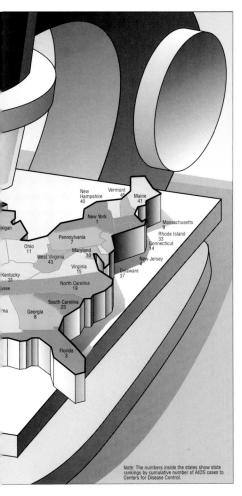

Note: The numbers inside the states show stste rankings by cumulative number of AIDS cases to Centers for Disease Control.

```
State Funding for AIDS Programs, FY 198!
            (Excluding Medicaid)

   State Funding Exceeds Federal

   California - 2
   Connecticut - 14
   Florida - 3
   Massachusetts - 9
   Minnesota - 23
   New York - 1
   Rhode Island - 33
   South Carolina - 25
   Washington - 12

   Ratio of Federal to State
   Spending is 2:1 to 1:1

   Alaska - 44
   Georgia - 8
   Hawaii - 28
   Illinois -6
   Kansas - 34
   Maryland - 10
   Michigan - 16
   Mississippi - 32
   New Jersey - 4
   Pennsylvania -7

   Ratio of Federal to State
   Spending is 5:1 to 2:1

   Alabama - 24
   Delaware - 37
   Indiana - 26
   Kentucky - 31
   Louisiana - 13
   Maine - 41
   Missouri - 18
   New Hampshire - 40
   New Mexico - 38
   Ohio - 11
   Oklahoma - 27
   Oregon - 22
   Utah - 36
   Virginia - 15
   Wisconsin - 29

   New Mexico - 38
   Ohio - 11
   Oklahoma - 27
   Oregon - 22
   Utah - 36
   Virginia - 15
   Wisconsin - 29

   Ratio of Federal to State
   Spending is greater than 5:1

   Arizona - 20
   Colorado - 17
   Nevada - 30
   Tennessee - 21
   Texas - 5

   No State Funding
```

1. This is part of the state data I received from the art director.

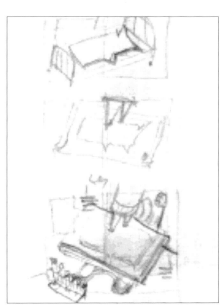

2. Even in a small thumbnail you can usually determine whether you're going to be able to fit all of your information into your picture. I knew from looking at the bottom conception that I could.

3. Instead of drawing a new U.S. map, I found a suitable one in my archive files.

These copies are workhorses—they serve as templates of the world, the U.S., Canada, the continents, and other areas; you just copy the template into a new illustration file and begin. I found a suitable map (3), but instead of placing it into a new FreeHand file, as I'd normally do, I put it into Adobe Dimensions (4).

Dimensions can be described—although far too summarily—as a 3-D special effects program. Let's say you draw an image in flat, straight-on two dimensions. You can then do various manipulations to the image, such as lighting or extruding selected objects in the illustration.

At this point we have a new Dimensions file open with the map outline on it. Now the fun—I should say the sport—begins. (I'm just learning the program as of Spring 1994, experimenting with the different features and settings.)

A tricky task must be solved first. I need to figure out how to align the image to get the proper angle of perspective for the illustration. First, I use the rotating and revolving tool to adjust the x, y, and z axis settings (4). In the dialog box, I adjust the horizontal axis minus sixty degrees, which tilts the image back in its 3-D space (4).

This seemed an interesting orientation, but I wanted to experiment. I thought I'd give one of Dimensions' built-in perspectives a whirl. It has

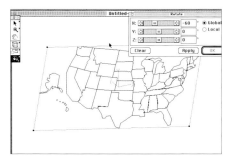

4. I placed the map, minus the color, in Adobe Dimensions, a 3-D program. First I tilted the horizontal axis minus 60 degrees.

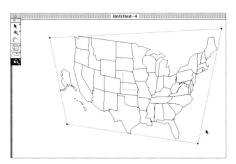

5. I tried one of Dimension's built-in perspectives. This was a little too off-the-wall.

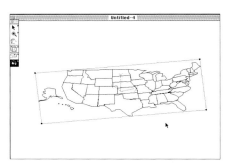

6. The third setting looked right ("angle: off-axis front" and "perspective: none").

7. The extrude command is selected from the Operations menu.

8. Extruding produces the "cliffs" along the U.S. border. The light source is now adjusted.

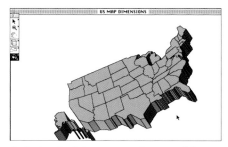

9. Setting the light source to the west of the country produces these highlights and shadows on the cliffsides.

many choices, including front, back, top, and bottom; off-axis front, back, top, and bottom; wide-angle; no perspective (straight-on); and others. I chose "view angle: front" and "perspective: wide angle" (5). Not a pretty sight.

The next combination: "angle: off-axis front" and "perspective: none." This tilted the map back far enough that it seemed to have the right orientation to rest on a slide under a microscope (6).

EXTRUDING AMERICA

Now it's time to tell Dimensions to "extrude" the map outline—that is, the program extends an image out into a third dimension (7). The orientation of the extrusion is governed by the 2-D image's angle and perspective.

The extruded map shape is shown in Figure 8, with the third dimension represented by the coastal contour cliffs. The inset dialog box shows the position of the light source (the small white square at the top left of the globe). The result of setting the light source is shown in Figure 9.

What this simple extrusion has done is save me a huge amount of time which otherwise would have to be spent drawing each of the cliffside rectangles in a drawing program like Aldus FreeHand or Adobe Illustrator, or—this is inconceivable to me now—by hand.

At any rate, along with other tasks like positioning type, I still needed to add the graduated fills to these cliffside rectangles to give them natural-looking highlights and shadows. So I took the extruded map out of Dimensions and back into FreeHand (10). (These inter-program transactions are quick and painless, for the most part.)

Back in FreeHand, the map file is opened, and the map is rotated to the exact angle needed to sit on the microscope slide (11).

In order to fill the cliffside blocks with highlights and shadows, I select all of them and group them (12). They're all given a standard graduated fill, such as "60% grey to

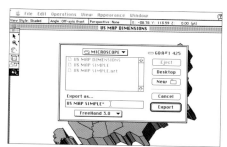

10. The map is exported out of Dimensions and back into FreeHand.

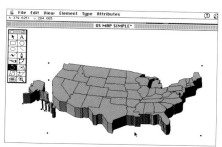

11. The map has to be turned clockwise with the rotating tool so that it will line up with the microscope slide it sits on.

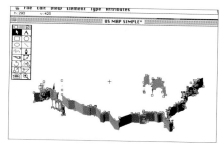

12. The "cliffside" rectangles are all selected so that they can be uniformly given a graduated fill from grey to white.

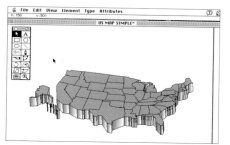

13. Fills in the individual rectangles are adjusted to get the lights and shadows right.

white." Then, one by one, I make minor adjustments to the percentages in order to render selected areas in greater or lesser shadow (13).

The final is shown in Figure 14.

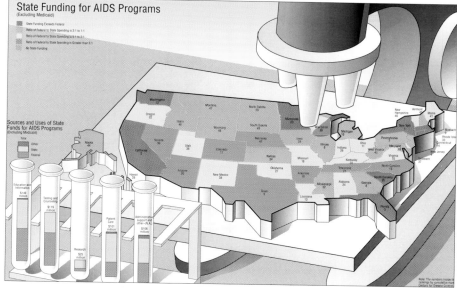

14. The final illustration.

Staying On Track

Charting Stock Option Prices

I was approached by Inc Design, a New York design firm. They wanted me to do a chart for a publication of Merck & Co.

For several consecutive years, Merck & Co. has been selected by the readers of *Fortune* magazine as America's most admired corporation

One of the things Merck does right, presumably, is to encourage and make it possible for employees to be owners of the company.

To celebrate the centennial of the company's existence, Merck set up a stock option grant for employees. An article in the company magazine would explain the option, and a chart was needed to show the value of the stock option as of September 6, 1992, and a comparable date for each of the 11 preceding months.

In spite of the impressive long-term growth of the company, and the very high regard in which it is held by Wall Street analysts, Merck seems to me very careful not to toot its own horn very much. Especially not to employees–they know what's going on, anyway.

The Merck management decided (as I imagine) not to make the article on the stock option grant a blue-sky affair, with bountiful rewards promised at the end of the rainbow—but rather an explanation of a

CLIENT: Inc Design
TIME: 6 hours
SIZE: 363k
PROGRAM: FreeHand

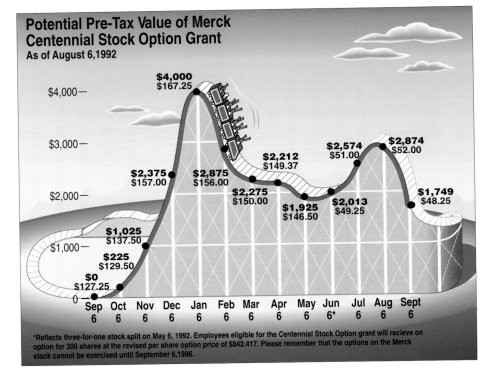

Potential Pre-Tax Value of Merck Centennial Stock Option Grant
As of August 6,1992

*Reflects three-for-one stock split on May 6, 1992. Employees eligible for the Centennial Stock Option grant will recieve on option for 300 shares at the revised per share option price of $842.417. Please remember that the options on the Merck stock cannot be exercised until September 6,1996.

conservative investment decision.

Accordingly, the chart I was hired to do would have three primary functions. First, it would, if successful, attract the attention of an employee who was reading, or skimming through, the company magazine. Second, it would show the information—the value of the stock option—clearly and accurately.

Third, and perhaps most importantly (again, my guess), it would present the information in a way that would imply the volatility of the option, the extreme swings in the value of the option over a one-year period.

It would need to do it in a relatively light-hearted way, compared to the very plain and serious way such

numbers might be shown in an annual report.

It was very important that the option holders—Merck employees—be comfortable with, at least not lose sleep over, the fact that the value of their options would have ups and downs, sometimes major swings.

DEVELOPING THE ILLUSTRATION

This project, like most of my chart projects, was going to pose the perplexing question: What is the appropriate image for this chart?

I wanted a symbol that would serve as a visual vehicle for showing the ups and downs of the value of the option on different dates. But I didn't want to use a traditional fever

> **"When you were a kid, if you were good at manipulating the cartoon images you "transferred" onto Silly Putty, you'll probably do OK with curve handles."**

chart, with straight lines connecting the numerical values and forming a jagged chart line. That would be too reminiscent of a conventional stock price chart.

Something fresher was needed, something a little more fluid-looking, something that didn't suggest—jagged movements! I ruminated about this at various times over several days (I'm usually working on 6 or 8 things simultaneously); but then the Inc Design art director solved the problem for me by suggesting that I use a roller coaster for the chart symbol. Why didn't I think of that?

Well, it was time to get on track. The art director had sent me a line chart with the numbers plotted (1), and the first thing I wanted to do was to see whether these numbers would lend them themselves to underpinning a roller coaster track. I drew a highly refined thumbnail (2) that suggested a goodness-of-fit. Then it was time to face the screen.

As the first step, I plotted the stock option values on the y-axis, the x-axis nodes representing the successive points in time. Working in FreeHand, you have to draw bars, using the rectangle tool, rather than just place points on the illustration window to create a line.

FreeHand won't save a freeform line as a group—that is, it won't freeze the position of the line on your x-y grid in the illustration window (in FreeHand terminology, the line "ungroups" itself). Each time

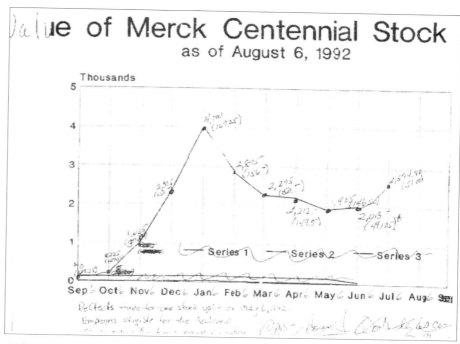

1. The art director supplied these numbers.

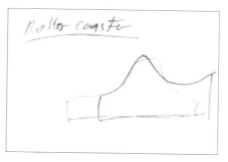

2. Based on a very rough thumbnail plotting, I decided that the roller coaster image would work.

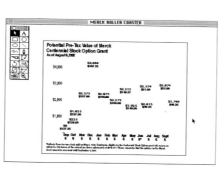

3. Using the rectangle tool, I drew bars to the precise height of each of the numerical values.

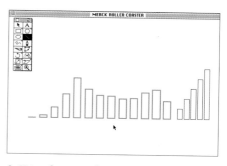

4. I placed the type above, below, and to the side of the bars, putting it on its own layer, the "type layer."

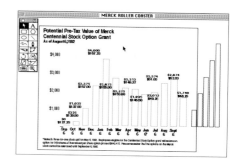

5. I superimposed the type layer on the layer with the bars, and was ready to connect the numbers and draw the chart line.

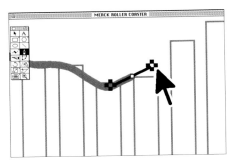

6. I pushed up on the right curve handle, which deepened the arc of the curve segment coming into the curve point that the handles are attached to.

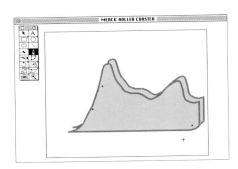

7. I made a closed polygon out of the outline of the track and supporting structure. I cloned the polygon and slightly offset it.

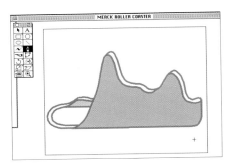

8. This yielded the two sliver-like paths which now can be filled with the cross-ties.

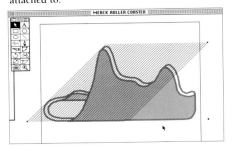

9. I power-duplicate a bunch of parallel diagonal lines.

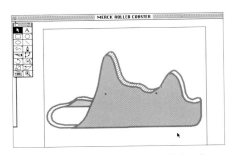

10. Then I cut and paste them inside the slivers.

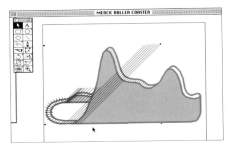

11. The ties for the curving part of the track had to be drawn individually. Normally I'd use the FreeHand rotating tool, but this was actually quicker to do by hand.

you open the illustration file, you'll have to reposition the line to its proper place on your scale.

The solution is to draw bars—closed polygons—ending them at their respective point values (3). Closed polygons are groupable elements in FreeHand, whose positions you can freeze, both relative to the grid and to each other.

On another layer, after I finished plotting the numbers, I placed the type at positions above or below their corresponding numerical value points (4). Then I made the two layers visible, one on top of the other, so that I could draw the line connecting the numbers—the line that would form the base of the track (5).

HANDLING CURVES

To build this line, I used the pen tool: I clicked on the top left corner of each bar, then held the mouse down and dragged to approximate the curve to the next bar, where I clicked again to place another curve point. I then fine-tuned each curved segment by adjusting the clover-like curve handles which are attached to each curve point.

Look at the close-up in Figure 6. By "pushing up" the curve handle on the right, with the mouse doing the controlling and the pointer doing the metaphorical pushing, I deepen the dip of the curve segment before that point.

Without a doubt, the most diffi-

cult-to-learn and subtle aspect of FreeHand is the fine-tuning of curves by the manipulation of "curve handles." The technical manuals on using FreeHand spend quite a bit of time on curve-handle manipulation, but it's the sort of dynamic eye-hand-mind skill, like playing one of the car-racing arcade games, that you just have to spend hours—many hours—getting the feel for. When you were a kid, if you were good at manipulating the newspaper cartoon images you "transferred" onto Silly Putty, you'll probably do OK with curve handles.

After I finished connecting and curving the chart line, I continued this line to make the rest of the foreground coaster track; then I continued this line to the ground and connected it to the other end, making it a closed polygon (7). This polygon would outline the supporting truss of the coaster track, which I'll soon be filling up with girders and beams. For now, I filled it with a solid grey.

First, though, I'll clone this polygon and move the clone so that it's slightly offset to the original (7). This will yield two sliver-like closed paths which, after some curve-handle manipulation and line editing, will give the top of the coaster track a little oblique perspective (8).

CUTTING AND PASTING

Now that we have the shapes of the structure, we can start putting in all the ties, girders, and beams needed to hold the whole thing up.

Let's start by adding the cross-ties to the top part of the track. By drawing a diagonal line and power-duplicating it a number of times, you generate a bunch of parallel diagonals (9). Then we cut these lines, using the track shape as a cookie-cutter, and paste them inside the track shape (10).

To make the cross-ties on the bottom left segment of the track, I used some more of the diagonal lines. But I also had to draw—individually—the lines for the "radial" ties in the 180 degree turn of the track (11).

Now it's time to add the truss structure which holds up the track and cars. I start by drawing the two thick vertical and horizontal I-beams, and one column of the diag-

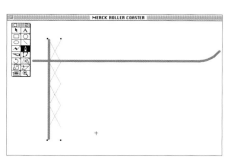

12. The truss structure is started by drawing the two thick vertical and horizontal I-beams, and one column of the diagonally latticed struts.

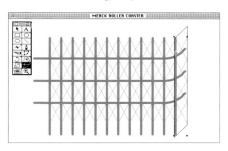

14. Skewing the last cloned section makes it appear to curve away from the reader's point of view.

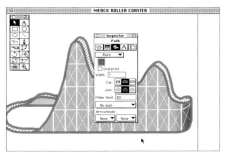

16. FreeHand, like other illustration programs, makes it a snap to set or modify line weights.

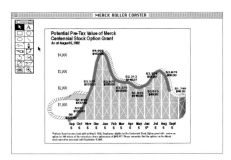

18. The type is brought up from a lower layer to the top one.

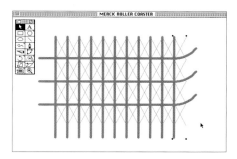

13. Cloning these elements fills out most of the truss.

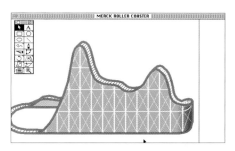

15. Electronic masking, using the "cut" and "paste inside" commands, puts the truss inside the outline.

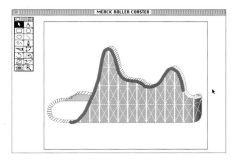

17. The thick red 7-point line. The chart line now will stand out a little.

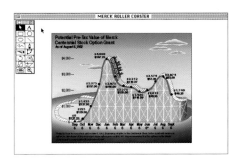

19. The final image. The landscape is on a lower layer than the coaster.

onally latticed beams (12). I clone the horizontal beam twice, then clone the vertical section 10 times, which yields almost all the truss structure (13).

Almost. The last partition of truss beams at the right need to be made to curve around the rear. The way to do this is to take the last clone I made and select it (shown by the four "element handle" points in Figure 13), and then skew it with the skewing tool (14). This slants the element vertically to create the necessary visual distortion.

The next job is to take this truss pattern and put it in the irregular polygon I created earlier (8). You do this in two steps. First, you cut the pattern (the "background element," in FreeHand terminology) with the polygon shape (the "clipping path"). Then you choose the "paste inside" command to paste the pattern precisely inside the polygon—this is like electronic masking (15).

A few finishing touches remain. We need to make the chart line more emphatic. If we go to the "Fill and line" dialog box and set the line weight to 7 points and specify the color as "red 100%/yellow 100%" (16), that should give us the bold red line we need (17).

We only need now to bring up the type layer and place it on top of the art layer, making a few slight adjustments so that numbers don't overlap the chart line (18). The final image shows the background and foreground landscaping which has been added on a lower printing layer so that it's under the coaster (19).

Ethereal Extrusion

Making A 3-D Bar Chart

Bank One Corporation, a fast-growing regional bank system based in Columbus, Ohio, needed a bar chart that would show, simply but in an attention-grabbing way, asset growth from 1973 to 1993.

Now, I'm basically a creative illustrator. I do bar charts that look like balloons and cliffs, pie charts that pose as tablecloths, and line charts that are portrayed as chains. I naturally steer away from the aggressively plain kinds, like the minimalist pie charts Ross Perot used for his TV presentations during the 1992 Presidential campaign.

True, these pies did help Perot serve up his message. But pedestrian pastries won't do for most clients. They're going to be interested in images that have pizzazz, surprise, creativity, even a little strangeness.

Financial clients—banks, insurance companies, investment institutions, and the like—are different. As a rule, they prefer charts to be clean and straightforward, sober and serious. Obviously, a great deal is at stake to the firm preparing an advertisement or annual report aimed at winning new customers or investors.

There seems to be a feeling among many financial clients that the less cleverly or creatively the information is charted, the more seriously it will

CLIENT: Bank One
TIME: 4 hours
SIZE: 143k
PROGRAM: Dimensions;
** FreeHand**

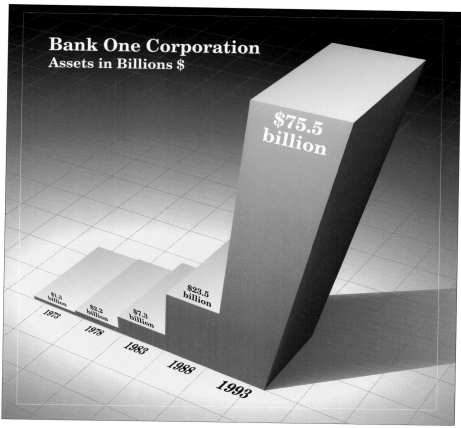

Bank One Corporation
Assets in Billions $

$75.5 billion

$23.5 billion

$1.3 billion 1973
$2.2 billion 1978
$7.3 billion 1983
1988
1993

be taken by the target readership. The catch is, if the chart is boring, it won't grab a reader's attention in the first place.

As an illustrator, you have to create something that's eye-catching, yet serious and ostensibly un-creative. You aim for a sort of Mount Rushmore graphic quality.

DEVELOPING THE ILLUSTRATION

I sent the client three samples: a bar chart with multi-colored bars (1), one of my self-promotion ads containing several charts (2), and a chart in a fake 3-D, or isometric, projection, whose bars resembled pieces of lumber (3). I should have

realized that the three bar charts in the first two samples would be considered too gaudy or too imaginative for portraying bank assets. They liked the third, the "lumber" chart. Could I do something like that, but in true perspective? The answer was yes.

To illustrate what he wanted, the art director sent me a rough—a bar chart in three-point perspective (4), along with the numbers for the chart (5). Then I sat down at the Mac.

Basically, it was a three-part operation. First, in FreeHand, I drew the 2-D chart bars (6). Then I exported the chart into a 3-D rendering program, Adobe Dimensions, and

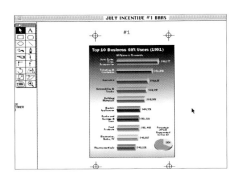

1. This chart with its multi-colored 3-dimensional bars was considered a little too gaudy a style for the present illustration.

4. The art director did this rough—a 3-dimensional bar chart with 3-point perspective—and faxed it to me.

"extruded" it into "solid" bars (7-13). Finally, I brought the chart back into FreeHand and did some finishing work (14).

After I drew the chart (6), I skewed it (7) with FreeHand's skewing tool to set the angle for the oblique perspective that Dimension would give it. Then I exported the image from FreeHand and placed it

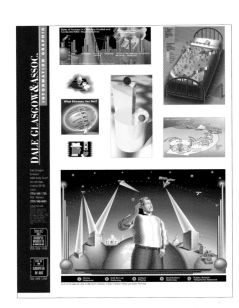

2. I sent the client this self-promotion ad containing several charts. They were all too creative for the data to be presented here: bank assets.

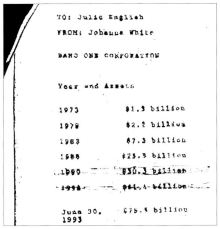

5. These are the numbers for the chart. Notice the deletion of the data for 1990 and 1991: it was decided to keep to a quinquennial interval for the chart, for the period 1973 to 1993.

into Dimensions, where it became a new illustration file.

A 3-D EXTRUSION

Adobe Dimensions is a 3-D modeling and rendering program. You can, as I did here, draw something in Aldus Freehand or Adobe Illustrator, export the image into

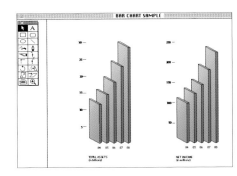

3. I also sent this chart, with its pieces of lumber (bars) shown in isometric projection. The client wanted to go in this direction, but in true perspective.

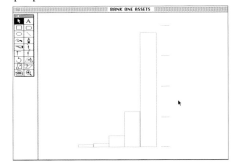

6. I drew the 2-dimensional chart in FreeHand.

Dimensions, and apply 3-D effects to it, such as turning, lighting, or extruding. Then you can export your image out of Dimensions and back into your illustration program.

It's important to understand that when you export an image from Dimensions and import it into FreeHand, for example, you have a real working drawing.

Since the Dimensions image is in the PostScript page description language, all the points of the image are active: that is, FreeHand recognizes the image as one of its own kind, an object that it can edit.

(By contrast, other 3-D programs like Infini-D, which have their own

" You aim for a sort of Mount Rushmore graphic quality. It's not easy. "

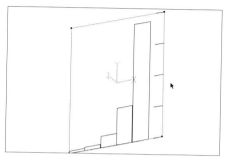

7. Using the skewing tool, I angled the chart to set up the perspective that would be rendered when I imported it into Dimensions.

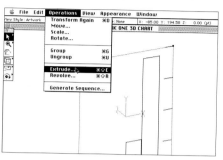

8, 9. In order to turn the 2-D bars into 3-D bars, I selected the Extrude feature in Dimensions, and set it to a depth of 100 points.

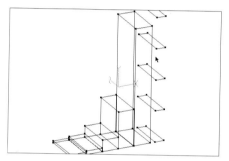

10. The extruded chart. The horizontal chart lines are now rectangles, and the bars are now solid boxes. The five rectangles lined up at the right are the scale markers (20 billion, 40 billion, etc.)

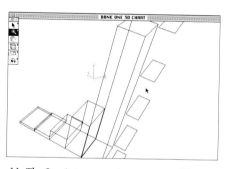

11. The 3-point perspective was created by rotating and skewing the extrusion to the appropriate vantage point.

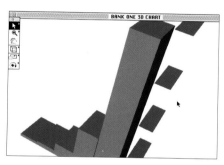

12. The final image in Dimensions. The boxes—actually, more like four buildings and a skyscraper—have been filled with color.

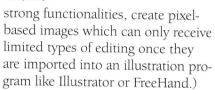

strong functionalities, create pixel-based images which can only receive limited types of editing once they are imported into an illustration program like Illustrator or FreeHand.)

Getting back to our chart, once it's in Dimensions we want to turn the 2-D bars into 3-D bars. To do this, you go to the Extrude dialog box in the Operations menu, and set the extrusion depth to 100 points (8, 9). What results is that the chart bars are now boxes (10).

The extrusion was rotated and skewed to the desired vantage point. This turned and gave perspective to the boxes (11). The final job in Dimensions was to colorize the

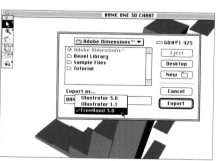

13. It's easy to export the file from Dimensions back into FreeHand. These programs really click, so to speak.

boxes (12). Then the file is exported from Dimensions into FreeHand.

Back in FreeHand, I inserted the type, and added the underlying grid and filled it with blends to create the highlight and backgrounds (14).

A bit of advice: when you're thinking about applying striking effects

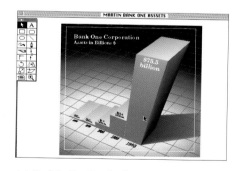

14. Back in FreeHand, after I added the type and the underlying grid, I put two highlighting blends on the grid: one from yellow to blue, the other from blue to dark blue; 100 steps in each.

like 3-D, it's important that substantial differences exist among the numbers. Otherwise, it can look comical because the chart bars are too similar in length or height. Fortunately, in the Bank One numbers, there was a progression from $1.3 billion in 1973 to $75.5 billion in 1993.

Prongful Acts

Fine-Tuning the Fork

It's always a challenge to find a suitable visual vehicle to carry a bar chart or pie chart.

By age 12 or 15 the average person has probably seen a thousand or more charts—all pretty much identical in form. When he encounters a new chart, chances are that there is no visual surprise to arrest his gaze and focus his attention on the information content of the chart.

You might say that inside every boring chart some interesting numbers are trapped, waiting to be freed from their eye-glazing form. It is one of the main jobs of the information illustrator to liberate the numbers, to create the visual surprise which draws the reader in.

I was hired by *Prevention* magazine to do a set of 6 charts which would illustrate key findings from a nationwide survey of women's health habits.

One set of survey questions asked women about their healthful dietary habits, whether they ate, for example, low-fat foods, high-fiber foods, and calcium-rich foods.

DEVELOPING THE ILLUSTRATION

I thought that a fork might be an interesting and appropriate symbol, with the fork prongs serving as the chart bars. Visual interest would be

CLIENT: *Prevention* magazine
TIME: 3.5 hours
SIZE: 250k
PROGRAM: FreeHand

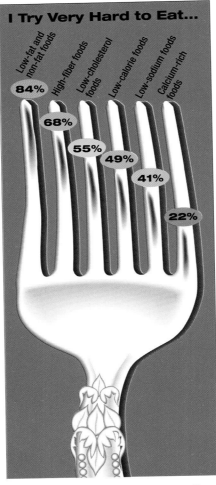

added by rendering a "reflective," smooth-metal surface.

After drawing the lengths of the bars which would be represented by the fork prongs (2), I superimposed them on an outline of the fork (3). In the upper part of each bar I placed the reflective shadow areas you'd see on a fork if you held it up to a light at the proper angle.

As I was doing this I realized that if the prongs were cut off at the chart bar tops, resulting in a tapered-prong fork, the image would

be more visually surprising, and the information would be more clearly presented as well (4).

The client decided against it, however, and chose to have all the prongs fully extended like a normal fork (5). In order to show the numbers clearly, different-colored ellipses are placed at the tops of the shadow areas.

Although I preferred the uneven-pronged fork, the client did have a point. Uneven prongs representing the chart bars might have given the impression that the illustration was primarily calling attention to the *differences* among the percentages, when in fact the article placed as much emphasis on the overall high level of healthy eating practices the survey found. At any rate, you ultimately have to go with your client's preferences.

It was a simple matter then to insert the typography. After entering the chart bar labels into the illustration file with the FreeHand text tool (6), the labels are rotated 60 degrees (7), and each label is positioned at the top of the appropriate prong (8).

The final image shows a close-up of the fork stem pattern, which was drawn with the pen tool, using a kitchen fork as a model (9).

Most of the elements, such as the 3 leaf petals in the middle, are based on single elements which were duplicated (9).

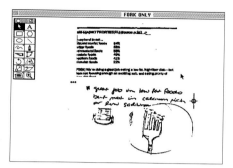

1. A fax from the client with thumbnails of my 2 conceptions: a plate and a fork.

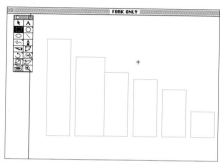

2. I drew the lengths of the chart bars which would then be pasted into the fork prongs.

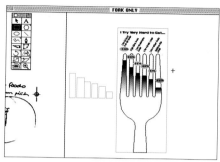

3. The first rough I faxed to the art director, showing the placement of the prong shadow areas, the ellipses, and the typography.

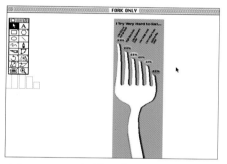

4. I came upon the idea of an uneven-pronged fork, which would've been more visually arresting, but the client decided on the full-length fork.

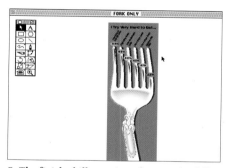

5. The finished illustration, showing the different-colored ellipses to present the numbers.

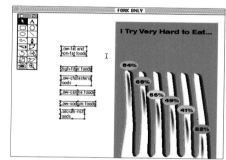

6. The chart bar labels are entered in with the text tool.

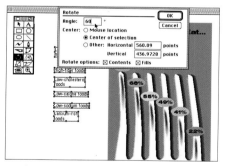

7. The rotation tool window, with the settings selected to rotate the labels 60 degrees.

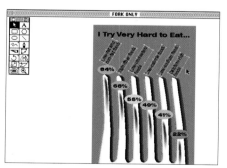

8. Each of the chart bar labels has been dragged into place at the top of a fork prong. They have all been rotated 60 degrees off their horizontal orientation.

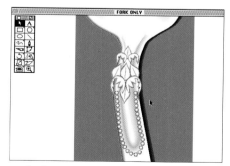

9. The fork stem pattern was drawn with the FreeHand pen tool at 200%. It's composed of a small number of basic elements which have been duplicated.

A Map of the Mall

A Monumental Undertaking

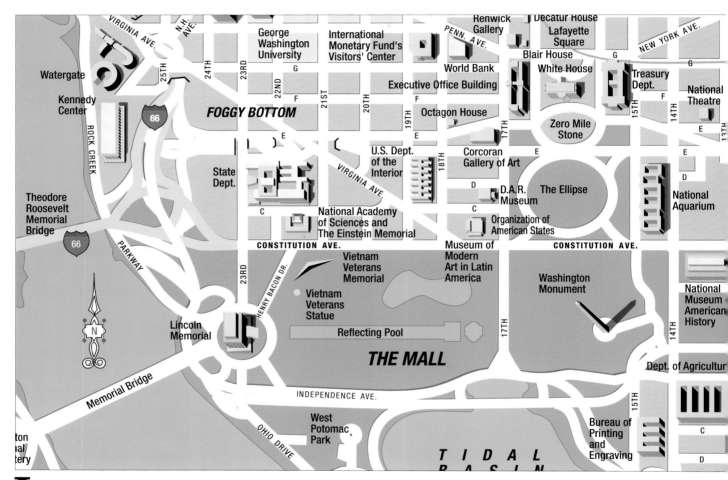

I like to do maps. They're quite challenging because they must show a great deal of information and they must show it clearly.

Streets, trains, rivers, parks, buildings, signs must all be presented accurately and in a format that doesn't make the reader squint or scratch his head in confusion—no small feat in itself, but a problem that's greatly compounded by the necessity to fit the type labels for all these things neatly into the picture. I guess I should say, I like it when I've *finished* a good map.

Bell Atlantic hired me to do the street maps for their annual *Visitor's Guide* to Washington, D.C. In this recon-struction we'll focus on the most complex of the maps, the one for the Mall area—Capitol, monuments, museums, and key Government buildings and other structures.

In many ways, the aspect of this project which may be most interesting to an illustrator concerns the reference material I relied on in drawing the map.

In order to construct a small-area map, such as a street map, you have to have reliable, up-to-date, and accurate images to use as the foundation for the layout. These can be one of several things. You might use a recently published map, if you can get permission from the copyright holders. Or you might be able to use older maps in the public domain—but they're apt to be out-of-date and inaccurate.

CLIENT: Bell Atlantic	SIZE: 1,200k
TIME: 45 hours	PROGRAM: FreeHand

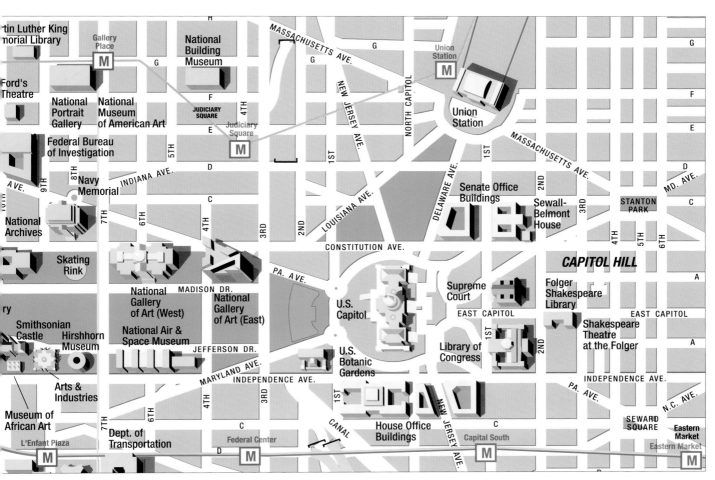

THE USGS—MOTHER LODE OF MAPPING RESOURCES

Fortunately, the U.S. Geological Survey (USGS) has come to the rescue. Using data and images which it and other cooperating agencies have compiled from aerial surveys of every square foot of the U.S., the USGS has produced massive photographic and cartographic databases that are available to the public through the National Mapping Program.

These databases include both digital images and photographs in various formats, such as line graphs, topographic maps, elevation models, land use maps, satellite image maps, and high-altitude photographs.

Of particular interest to map-making illustrators are the products of the National High Altitude Photography

Program (NHAP) and its successor, the National Aerial Photography Program (NAPP). The objectives of these programs are to develop a national photographic database covering the entire country, update the database regularly, and make the photographs easily available to any interested public or private user.

Both black-and-white and color infrared photographs are available. Each 9- by 9-inch black-and-white is at a scale of 1:80,000 (1 inch equals about 1.25 miles) and the color photos (same size) are at a 1:58,000 scale (1 inch equals 0.9 miles.) The important thing for us is that the photographs are of sufficiently high resolution that they can be enlarged to the size an illustrator needs, without losing significant detail. The USGS will, for prices ranging from $18 to $100 or more, prepare and send transparencies or photographic reproductions at the

1. The first reference picture was a high-resolution aerial photograph of the central D.C. area. I scanned it in.

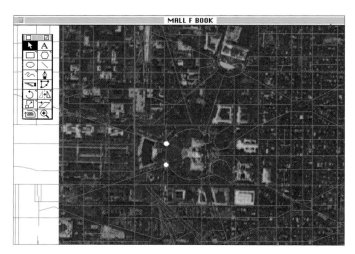

2. To make the tracing easier, I magnified and worked in one area of the scan at a time.

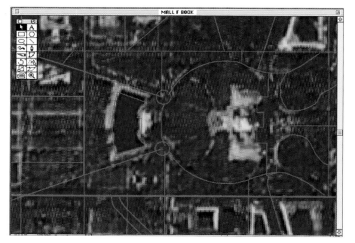

3. In each "work area," I traced over the street outlines of the scan.

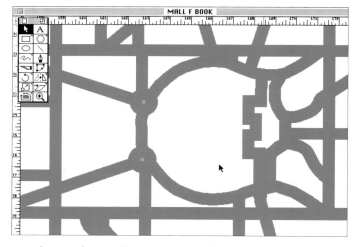

4. A close-up of some of the streets. I made them thicker than they actually appear on the scan, so that they'd be clearly visible and able to contain the type for the street names.

9- by 9-inch size, or at enlarged sizes (18 x 18; 27 x 27; or 36 x 36 inches).

As useful as these photographs are, they're not the last word. They're expensive, and they're time-consuming. You have to figure out what you want using the indexes; you have to order and wait; then you have to scan and trace. Then adjust your curve and corner points.

But wait—the USGS is aware of and concerned about these problems, and they have a really exciting product on the horizon: a CD-ROM presenting digital photo-images from the NAPP program. This disk, which USGS is working on (at Fall 1993), will contain images covering the entire U.S. at a scale of 1:40,000. When we get the disk (which probably will be reasonably priced), we'll be able to quickly find the image we want, download it into our drawing programs, and modify and use it as we please. (To get descriptive brochures, catalogs, indexes, and order forms, call the USGS National Cartographic Information Center at (703) 860-6045 or (800) 872-6277, or write: NCIC, c/o U.S. Geological Survey, Reston, VA 22092). Once you know which photograph you need, you can order it by phone or fax.)

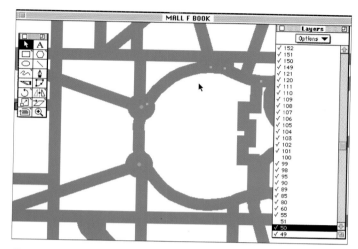

5. To give the streets a slight shadow, I colored them green . . .

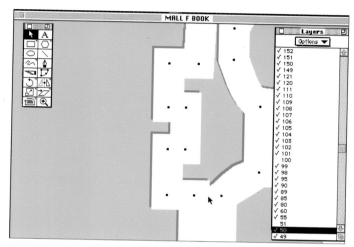

6. . . .then cloned them and colored the clone white.

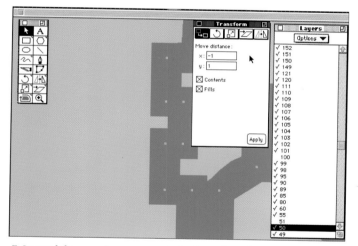

7. I moved the green layout one point horizontally and one point vertically. This slight offset created the thin green shadow lines.

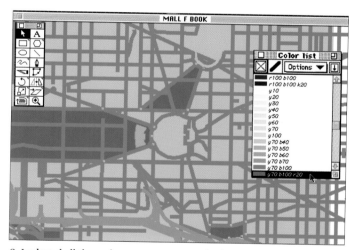

8. I selected all the park areas as a group and colored them a darker green.

DEVELOPING THE ILLUSTRATION

I ordered the black-and-white photograph covering the central Washington, D.C. area and part of northern Virginia. After I scanned in the photo covering the Mall area (1), I enlarged one part of the scan at a time (2).

Then, working in FreeHand on the "current drawing layer," I started tracing over the street outlines of the scan, which I'd put on a lower layer (3). Figure 4 shows a close-up of some of the streets surrounding the U.S. Capitol. These street lines are thicker than they actually are, so that they will be easier to see on the map, and also so that they'll be able to contain the street names.

I wanted the streets to have a slight shadow on their northern and western edges (for east-west streets and north-south streets, respectively.) To accomplish this I colored the streets green and put them on Layer 50 (5). Then I cloned the streets as a group, colored them white, and put them on Layer 51 (6).

Then I moved the green layout one point both horizontally and vertically to offset it very slightly down and to the right of the white layout (7), creating the thin green outlines (they're visible on the final image on the first two pages).

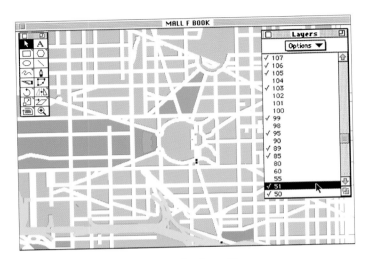

9. The finished street layout, assigned to Layer 51.

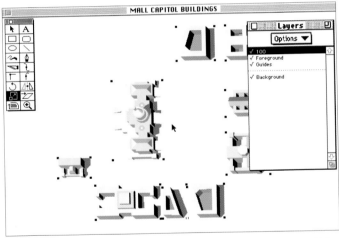

11. I started rendering buildings in an extremely simplified way—they'd be too small on the map for much detail. I slanted them in an isometric projection at 45 degrees.

To give the park areas their darker green, I selected all of them and filled them with 70% yellow/100% blue (8).

The finished street layout for the Capitol area, which I designated Layer 51, is shown in Figure 9. Now I'll bring in the group of buildings for this area from another file. Let's switch our attention to that file for a few moments.

THE BUILDINGS

I used various reference sources to help me in drawing the Mall area buildings. First, to nail down the overhead profiles—the outlines the map reader would see—I used

10. For one of my reference images, I took this photographic montage of some of the buildings in the Smithsonian Institution complex.

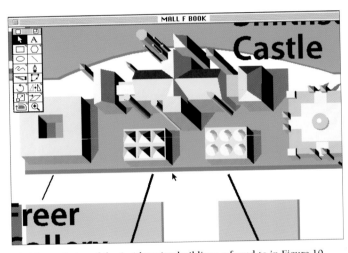

12. My rendering of the Smithsonian buildings referred to in Figure 10.

the scanned high-altitude photo (1), with individual buildings magnified 400% or more.

For the details of specific buildings, I relied on several sources. The most important was the photographic book *Above Washington*, by Robert Llewellyn. This outstanding work contains aerial photographs of hundreds of Washington, D.C.'s most famous and important buildings, with many of the structures shown from several vantage points.

Although my buildings would be greatly simplified, these photos gave me a good feel for the look of many of the structures. I also used National Archive and stock photos, and even took some of my own, such as the montage of some of the Smithsonian Institution buildings shown in Figure 10.

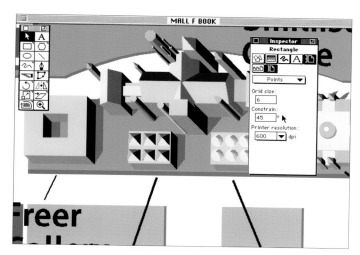

13. Using the FreeHand line tool and holding the shift key down while you draw the lines constrains them to a 45 degree angle off vertical.

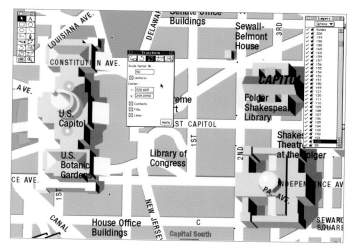

14. I brought the group of buildings—which I'd been drawing in a separate file to save processing and redrawing time—back into the map file. But they didn't fit. I had to scale them down 50 percent.

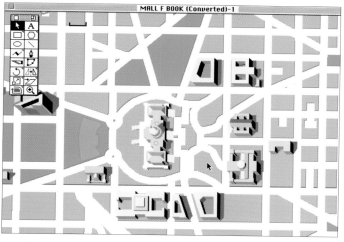

15. The Capitol area buildings now fit their street positions.

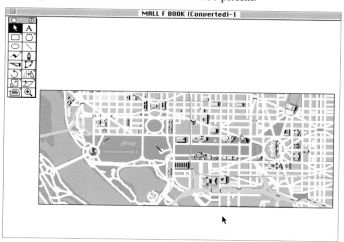

16. All the Mall buildings have been brought in from their work file, scaled down, and adjusted into correct positions.

Anyway, using the scan of the high-altitude photo (1) to get the overhead profiles and the street positions, I started drawing the buildings in a very basic, un-detailed style, not worrying about, or wishing to render, things like windows, columns, trees, or gardens (11). The buildings were cast in a simple, isometric perspective set at 45 degrees.

As an example, look at Figure 12. This is my rendering of the Smithsonian buildings I referred to above. After I drew the overhead view, the plan view, I drew the vertical lines for the buildings at a 45 degree slant (12). It was easy to do the lines at this angle, because when you draw straight lines with the FreeHand line tool and hold the

shift key down, it "constrains" the lines to 45 degrees off vertical, in the direction you move the mouse (13).

SEPARATE FILES OR SEPARATE LAYERS?

I didn't draw the buildings in the main illustration file ("Mall F Book"). Rather, I opened a new file, "Mall Capitol Buildings," to draw them in. Why did I draw the buildings in a separate file, rather than on a separate layer in "Mall F Book"?

I did it to save time—lots of time. Doing the buildings on layers in the main illustration file—which already had the streets laid out—would have made the file so large

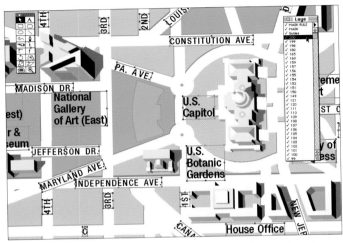

17. The type, which I'd kept out of the way on another layer, is brought in now and placed on top of the building and street layers.

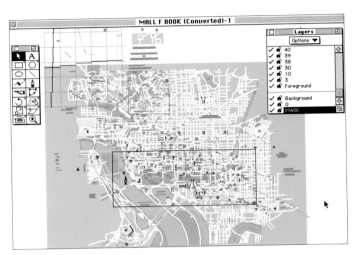

18. The Mall map was actually a part of a larger D.C. map I drew. The non-Mall areas have been masked out for the Mall map.

that the pace at which FreeHand processed my commands, and then redrew the screen, would become intolerably slow, producing a lot of dead time.

There's really no hard-and-fast rule about when a file is getting so large that some of the memory-intensive work is more efficiently done in separate files, then brought back into the main file. It depends on your system's size and speed, and your own tolerance.

Figure 11 shows one of the building groups done in the ancillary file. I designated the buildings as Layer 100, then placed it back into the main file.

Back in the main file, when I placed the group of buildings in their approximate position on the street layout, I found that they didn't fit—they were too big (14). I had to scale them down. Accordingly, I used FreeHand's scaling tool for the job (14).

Not only did I have to scale down the buildings to get them to fit; I also had to select various ones and move them around a little.

This is done by taking the pointer tool (the arrow in the top left corner of the toolbox) and moving it with the mouse until it's touching the object you want to move; then you just move it with your mouse.

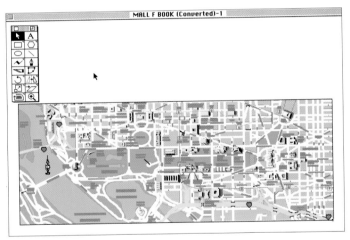

19. The final map.

Figure 15 shows the group of Capitol area buildings in their correct positions, and Figure 16 shows all the Mall buildings properly placed.

I had laid out the type on a separate Layer 200 which I made a background layer so that it wouldn't be visible, and wouldn't crowd the layout while I was bringing in the buildings and positioning them (17).

The final map is shown in Figure 19. It's actually just a part of the much larger D.C. map I drew (18), with all the non-Mall area masked out. The 20- by 30-inch "mega-map" was contained within the 40- by 40-inch printable area of a FreeHand illustration file. I sized the individual maps, such as the Mall map, individually, according to the size specifications I received from the client.

This map was a difficult, time-consuming job for me, but I knew that once I finished it, it would become a very important reference file in my personal image archives. Whenever I needed a map of the Mall, I could bring this file up and adapt it to use in other illustrations. So far I've used it, in modified form, in four other graphics, and saved the many hours it would have taken to make new maps from scratch.

Class Acts

Gamblers, Testers, Thinkers

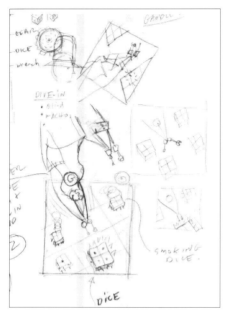

1. The thumbnails for the gambler. The bottom one was chosen.

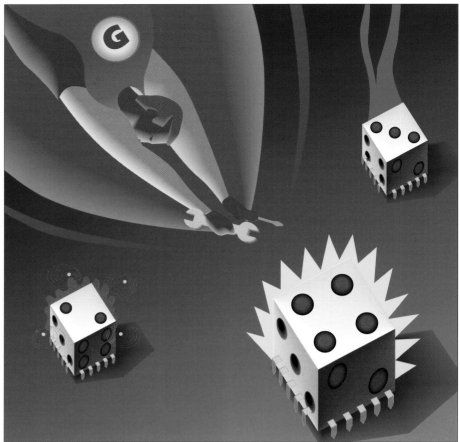

2. The final gambler. With the Superman-like motif, I tried to capture the gambler's plunge-right-in attitude.

CLIENT: ASTD *Journal*
TIME: 14 hours
SIZE: 2,650k
PROGRAM: FreeHand

Some of the illustrations I've most enjoyed doing were commissioned by the *Journal* of the American Society for Training and Development (ASTD).

These illustrations haven't been charts, maps, or technical diagrams—the three mainstays of my work. My drawings for ASTD, and for certain other clients, have been concerned primarily with portraying a different kind of information.

It may be instructive to look at the different types of facts an information illustrator works with. The aim is not to tell us how to treat each type graphically, of course; but perhaps we can broaden our view of our profession's subject matter.

WHAT IS AN INFORMATION ILLUSTRATION?

The information I'm given to illustrate usually is in one of three forms: statistics; processes or sequences; and classifications. Sometimes, of course, the information will imply an overlap of two or more of the forms: for example, a pie chart, each of whose slices represent data for one of the categories of a classification (such as budget programs, or causes of accidents).

Let's summarize these types of information and compare them. Certainly everyone will agree that a graphic which shows *statistical data*—a bar chart, pie chart, line chart, or table—constitutes an information illustration. The information is a bunch of numerical values, whose relationship to each other can be precisely determined because the scale of measurement is clearly indicated (if it isn't, it needs to be).

Analogously, a technical diagram also presents information. Whether it shows a complex *causal process,* a simple *sequence* of steps (such as exercise positions), or the detailed *structure* of something (a shark's insides; the Sun), a technical illustration shows the precise relationships of things to each other in space and time.

Many people consider statistical charts and maps and technical diagrams to entirely comprise an illustrator's scope of work. I don't so restrict myself. I also seek, and enjoy doing, illustrations whose main function is to visualize the categories of a classification. It was a classification that ASTD hired me to draw.

CLASSIFICATIONS

A *classification* is a logical set of groupings of things according to some characteristic. Types of ships, voters by party, classes of fabrics. Okay, fine, you might say, but is it information? In my view of the term "information," it is.

The term often seems to connote primarily a collection of facts, which may be numbers, steps, components, and so forth. In other words, a mass of particulars.

But you also need organizing frameworks to make sense out of a bunch of facts or observations; and one of the key logical frameworks we use is the classification. You group things together on the basis of similarities, and apart from other things with different characteristics.

In my view, an analytical framework such as a classification is inseparably related to the information that makes up the classes. It's needed to make sense of the information: to show the *logical* relationships—of similarity and difference—among things. That makes it proper material—and often very interesting material—for the information illustrator.

To sum up, I consider information illustration to be the precise graphic portrayal of facts and their numerical, spatial, temporal, causal, sequential, or logical relationships.

If you go along with the scope of this definition, then you'll agree that our field is by no means limited to charts, maps, and technical diagrams—even though they're probably everyone's bread and butter.

DEVELOPING THE ILLUSTRATION

ASTD had the text ready for an article which classified technical sys-

3. The tester thumbnails. The third was chosen; it had the best balance among the elements.

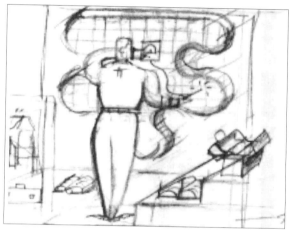

tems trouble-shooters into three categories: gamblers, testers, and thinkers. The text defined the behavior patterns associated with each primary category and its major subcategories. The text also explained the differences from the other two categories.

4. The final tester. The exaggerated puzzle piece stands up to the tester with his arsenal.

This article, intended primarily for persons who train or supervise technicians, is packed with complex, difficult concepts. It's well thought out and clearly written. But if you look at the fax of the typeset text the art director sent me, you'll see immediately how dense and formidable the article looks without illustrations. Both to help the reader keep in mind the three categories of trouble-shooters, and also to provide much-needed visual relief, I was asked to draw an illustration of each type.

The big difficulty with this project was the creative one: what images would I use, and how could I make them distinctly different while keeping a common sort of style throughout? I tried various conceptions for each trouble-shooter type.

THE GAMBLER

For the gambler, I conjured up one image which has a gambler sitting with a feather in his hat, an ace in one hand and a wrench in the other, looking at a die and a gear (1, top left). This didn't capture the reckless spirit of a gambler. Then I thought, how about a Superman motif—Mr. Supergambler with cape on his back and wrench in hand, zooming in toward several disturbed dice (1, bottom). The art director liked this idea and so did I. The gambler illustration is shown in Figure 2.

THE TESTER

I tried several ideas, which sort of evolved one to the next (3): a guy with a toolbox and a testing instrument; a guy with a technical manual; a guy with a toolbox, manual, and testing instrument, testing a small piece. The third had all the conceptual elements, but it was too cluttered.

I made the puzzle piece big like a TV game show marquee, so that it would dwarf the book and tools.

Then I added steps, to suggest the one-step-at-a-time, methodical nature of the tester.

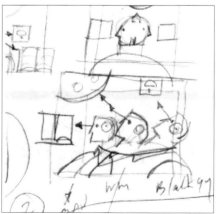

5. Doing the thumbnails for the thinker started making me see arrows and icons zooming around my own head.

6. The final thinker illustration. The caricatured symbolism of the first two images culminates here in the three-headed cogitator.

The final rendition of the tester is shown in Figure 4.

THE THINKER

The thinker was the preferred type of trouble-shooter. He processes all sorts of information—manuals, malfunctions, indicators, warning lights, his own experience, etc.—and works on it with his best tool: his analytical ability. I wanted to conjure up an image that suggested someone with multiple viewpoints or approaches.

After drawing several thumbnails featuring a cerebral face with arrows of activity buzzing around inside the brain, and surrounded by the icons (gears, testing machine, etc.), I tried out a three-headed figure, with multiple arrows and icons representing dynamic thought processes (5). This seemed to go along with the heavily symbolic style of the first two images, and was chosen.

The final image of the thinker is shown in Figure 6. Before we leave this project, let's do a little technical nitty-gritty. I decided that a round rainbow effect behind the heads and icons would help suggest several characteristics of the thinker: energy, harmony, and light. It would also be pleasing and help unify the different elements.

RAINBOWS AND PINSTRIPES

First I constructed three triangles—red, yellow, and blue—and juxtaposed them (7). Then I cloned each triangle and rotated the most clockwise point of the clone *counter-clockwise,* almost but not quite to the point where the two radial sides of each triangle would overlap (resulting in a ray).

You're left with three small slivers at the boundaries between the triangles (8). These slivers will be used as the blending elements, and the space between each two of them will get the nice smooth transition of colors; from yellow to blue, for example (9).

From out of the blended mega-triangle I cut out a circle, using FreeHand's cut and paste-inside tools (10, 11). I enlarged the circle and that was the rainbow.

To render the pinstripes that flow wavy over the rainbow, I also used a

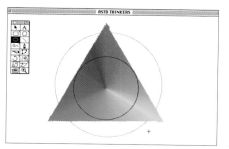

7. To render the rainbow, I made and juxtaposed triangles for the three primary colors.

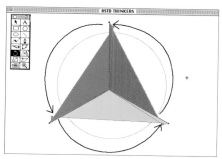

8. The three slivers at the triangle intersections will be the blending elements.

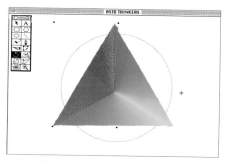

9. The blends produce the continuous gradation of colors.

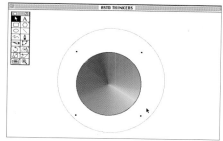

10, 11. I cut-and-pasted the rainbow blend inside a circle. The circle was put on a layer below the "person" and the symbols.

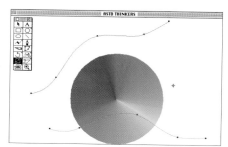

12. To render the undulating pinstripes superimposed upon the rainbow, I first drew two outer lines.

blend. I simply drew the two outer lines (12), then instructed FreeHand to execute a 20-step blend between them (13, 14), resulting in the pattern of lines that, to my eyes, add a little elegance and order to the composition (15).

Finally, the three sets of triple arrows were generated as one original and two clones. The set at the right (see the black arrow on the right in Figure 16) was produced with FreeHand's reflecting tool, which made a mirror image of the set at the left.

This really was a nice project. Since almost all of the laborious technical execution was done using basic FreeHand tools, I could let my energy flow into its preferred channel, creative problem-solving.

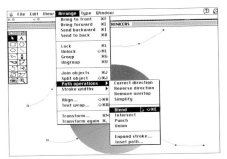
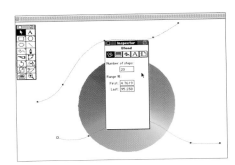

13, 14. These two lines formed the beginning and ending elements of a 20-step blend. The blend produced the 18 intermediate lines.

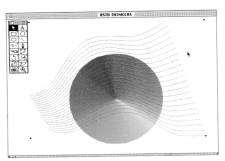

15. The blended pinstripes, over the rainbow.

16. The right set of arrows, whose curves have opposite arcs from the left set, was a reflected clone of the left set.

One Image, Three Programs

Photoshop, Infini-D, FreeHand

Although the majority of the illustrations discussed in this chapter were created using FreeHand, one shouldn't infer that this is the be-all and end-all of graphics software. It simply is the program I started with, and I have found that as I've gotten better and as FreeHand has been steadily improved, it remains easy-to-use and powerful, affording most of the functionality I need from a drawing program.

But there are many instances in which I've been able to create a much better illustration by executing certain aspects of the image in different programs.

1. Of the many references I had, this and the following NASA photograph were the two most important.

2. This photograph served as my chief model.

3. My laborious hand rendering of the full moon, done on grey board with colored pencils.

I actually use three types of drawing programs:

1) Object-oriented programs, such as Aldus FreeHand and Adobe Illustrator.

2) Image enhancement and manipulation programs like Adobe Photoshop and Fractal Painter.

3) 3-D rendering and special effects software, especially Specular International's Infini-D and Adobe Dimensions.

Although each of these programs competes with some of the others in various respects, the good news for the electronic illustrator is that programs in each category complement the ones in the other categories. Plus, in most cases they work together well.

This is true partly because a new software package written for the Macintosh has to be compatible with other Mac programs, to the greatest extent possible. Many of the commands, names of the features and tools, menus, and dialog boxes are similar or identical; and the ways you import and export files among programs are standardized and easy to learn.

In the discussion that follows, we'll look at a rendering of the seven phases of

CLIENT: *New Webster's Illustrated Dictionary*
TIME: 17 hours
SIZE: 30, 100k
PROGRAM: Photoshop, Infini-D, FreeHand

the moon (not counting the invisible new moon), which I did for *New Webster's Illustrated Dictionary.*

To summarize the progress of the illustration, I started with pencil and paper, then took the hand drawing into Photoshop and manipulated it, then took that image into Infini-D and added 3-D effects, and finally put it into FreeHand in order to add type and some ancillary images. Well, let's begin.

DEVELOPING THE ILLUSTRATION

The client had a requirement for the illustrations that would go into its *Dictionary*: none of the art would be based upon images traced over scanned photographs. I think the editors subscribed to the famous aesthetic first principle of Ezra Pound: "Make it new."

I find this requirement quite admirable. Everything in the book would be new, freshly rendered. Of course, it does make for a stiffer challenge to the illustrator. It meant that I had to draw the moon by hand. I left my Macintosh and embarked on an odyssey back in time, back to the old drawing board.

Of course, I did use reference pictures. Spreading out several dozen photos of the moon all over the carpet in my studio, I studied and compared, and

> **"A sampling of filter names might be suggestive: blur, noise, wave, sharpen, crystallize, spherize, emboss, pointillize, twirl, extrude, zigzag. "**

4. Applying the "find edges" filter accentuated the boundaries of contrast between bright areas and darker areas.

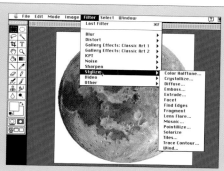

5. Photoshop has an extensive library of filters. This is one filter menu (users can customize their own), plus some of the specific filters in the stylize filter submenu.

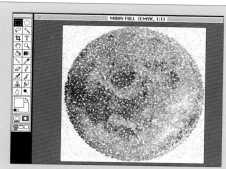

6. Trying out different filters, we start with the one that pointillizes.

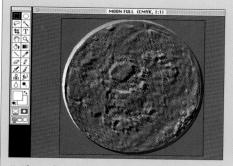

7. The emboss filter appears to add relief to the moonscape.

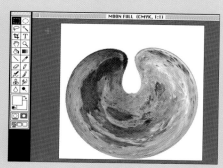

8. The polar coordinates filter changes the coordinates of an image from the conventional rectangular basis.

9. I make the dark side of the moon by "burning" in shadows with the Wacom electronic stylus as my brush.

finally settled on two NASA photos taken during the Apollo 11 mission as my chief references (1, 2). The second was my primary model.

On a piece of grey board, using white and dark brown pencils, I rendered my full moon (3). It took twelve hours, and the high resolution color scan at 2400 dpi consumed 27 megabytes. I imported the scan into Aldus FreeHand.

(One might wonder how to shuffle a 27-megabyte file around from designer to scanner, back to designer, and finally to service bureau—when the finished file had grown to over 30 megabytes! You need a large capacity disk. For this illustration the kind I used, one which has become an industry standard, is the SyQuest. It holds 44 megabytes and is roughly the size of a compact disc. Various companies sell SyQuest drives—including

SyQuest itself—and they don't differ too much in quality, so it pays to shop around in Mac catalogs and *MacUser* ads for the best price. SyQuest disks are priced in the $50-75 range, as of Spring 1994. The drives run from $300-$500.)

FILTERS AND SHADOWS

In Photoshop I wanted to do two things: enhance the scanned drawing by applying some of the program's filters; and paint onto the full moon image the varying shadows necessary to render the images for the seven phases of the waxing, waning, and full moon.

Photoshop's filters produce effects similar to the familiar photographic filters in common use. But Photoshop has, in addition, many filters that produce surprising, stunning, even strange results—filters without traditional photographic counterparts. A sampling of filter names

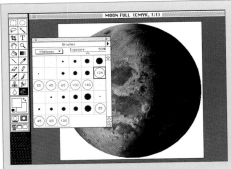

10. Photoshop's paintbrush grid has many standard diameters. . .

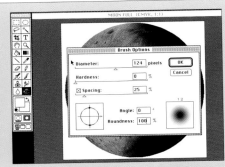

11. But you can customize your own brushes, as I did here, choosing one with a diameter of 124 pixels.

12. Finally the brightness and contrast are turned up. Now it's time to move over to Infini-D.

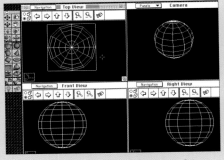

13. In Infini-D, we first generate a wire-frame sphere with the sphere tool.

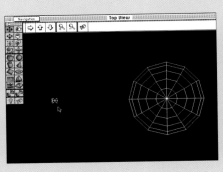

14. Next we change the light source. We make adjustments in both the top view and front view windows.

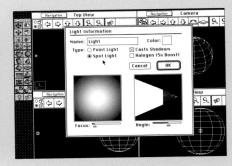

15. Spot lighting is selected.

might be suggestive: blur, noise, wave, sharpen, crystallize, spherize, emboss, pointillize, twirl, extrude, zigzag.

The filter menu and some of the individual filters in one submenu are shown in Figure 5. (You can customize your own filter menu, adding "modules" of filters that you commonly use. Specialized filters are marketed by Adobe and third parties.)

In order to brighten up the full moon image, I selected the "find edges" filter. This filter finds the transitional boundaries between bright and dark areas, and also between colors, and accentuates them by drawing light lines on the boundaries. Applying the filter to the image produced the effect shown in Figure 4.

I realize that I might have tantalized you with this talk about wild and crazy filters. Let's leave our moon with its

found edges (4) for a minute, and conjure up some meta-moons with other filters. Selecting the "stylize" filter submenu (5), we first choose the pointillize filter, which produces the curiosity resembling a weird tissue culture (6).

The emboss filter gives us the 3000-year-old Etruscan coin in Figure 7. The pelvis from an unknown creature is the effect of applying the polar coordinates filter to the poor moon (8). Lunacy.

Enough of these cheap thrills. Needless to say, when you use the filters seriously and creatively, you can accomplish image enhancements or manipulations you may not have thought possible, especially if you are new to electronic illustration and image retouching.

Let's get back to our project. It's time to render one of the moon phases, which I think is the "waxing gibbous"

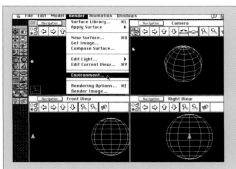

16. Infini-D's background ambient lighting is called the "environment."

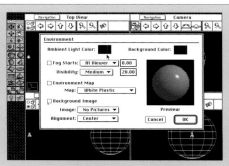

17. These are the current environment settings.

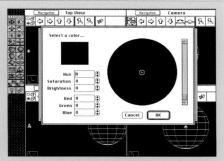

18. We want to turn off all color and light, so that there will be no ambient light. The moon has a very small amount of ambient light around it (from the earth and stars), but not enough to add any humanly visible brightness to the blackness of space.

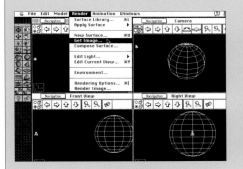

19. To bring in the moon phase images we choose "get image" from the Render menu.

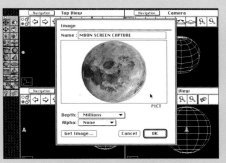

20. The images have been saved as PICT files; now they're opened in Infini-D.

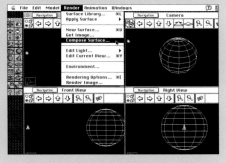

21. The moon phase image is a surface that Infini-D can compose onto one of the wire-framed spheres.

(this is just one of seven phases; the same basic technique is used for each one). Using the Wacom electronic stylus, and applying brush strokes to its electronic tablet, I "burn" shadows to create the dark side of the moon (9).

The brush settings are shown in Figures 10 and 11. The "124" refers to the diameter of the brush in pixels. This was a custom brush diameter I selected (11); you can also use standard Photoshop brushes (10). The last action in Photoshop is to turn up the overall brightness and contrast of the image (12).

To render the other moon phase images, I made a copy of the full moon image after having applied the "find edges" filter (4). Then I burned in the appropriate shadow in each one, using the Wacom stylus and tablet (9). When all the phase images were finished with Photoshop, I exported their file into the 3-D program, Infini-D.

INFINI-D

Infini-D is a 3-D modeling and rendering program from Specular International. In a nutshell, it enables you to:

1) Create basic "generic primitive" shapes like spheres, cubes, or cylinders, or custom shapes, such as vases, car bodies, and tables.

2) Apply surfaces to the shapes you create. A surface can be one of Infini-D's many ready-made textures, or a texture you create in Infini-D, or an image you've created elsewhere and wish to map onto a shape. This last is what we'll be doing.

3) View your object from any camera angle, and position single or multiple light sources in relation to your object.

22. The dialog box for setting up the surface composition.

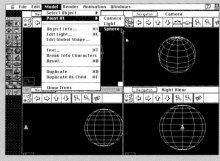

23. The light source is pointed directly at the globe.

24. The almost-halfmoon is rendered by the ray trace tool.

4) Construct animated sequences of images, showing your object moving or changing in time.

For our moon shots, we'll be involved with the first three of these functions. The first step is to create a sphere shape, using the sphere tool highlighted in the palette (13). All you do is drag the rectangle box and the program generates the wire-frame sphere to fit it.

Infini-D gives you four standard windows—viewpoints through which you can see your object: top view, camera, front view, and right view. You can adjust the camera to any position. (You could also choose a left view, bottom view, or other views. They're not needed here.)

Next I want to change the light source. I look at the top view to find the light source (the small symbol the arrow's pointing at) and move it to the left side of the drawing. I also adjust it vertically in the front view.

This will be a single light source, representing the sun, casting its rays from the left of the moon (14). Then the light type is set: spot is chosen (15). To complete the lighting

adjustments we have to change the "environment" (16)—the default ambient light existing in the scene—and get rid of it completely (17). Now there's almost no ambient light around the moon (18).

Figure 17 shows the current environment settings, along with a preview window which shows what a generic sphere looks like with the ambient light. In the dialog box in Figure 18, all the color and light parameters are turned down to zero: no ambient light.

PUTTING IT ALL TOGETHER

Finally we can go get our moon phase images (19) and map them onto the spheres. The images, for example the full moon, currently reside as Photoshop documents. They're imported as PICT files (20).

We take each moon phase image, with the surface and shadows we've manipulated in Photoshop, and compose this surface onto one of our Infini-D spheres (21).

The surface composition dialog box is shown in Figure 22. The window at the right previews what

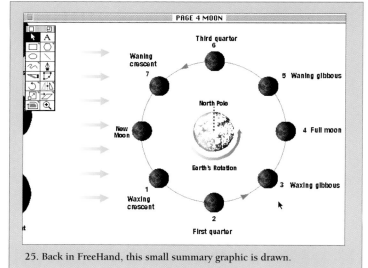

25. Back in FreeHand, this small summary graphic is drawn.

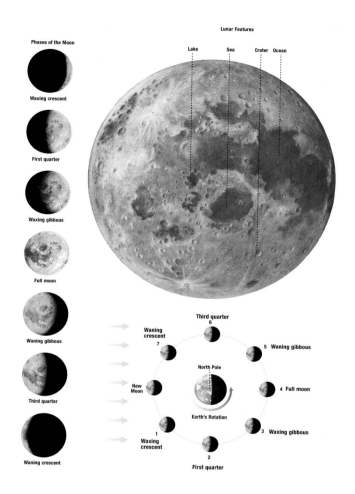

Lunar Features

Lake   Sea   Crater   Ocean

Phases of the Moon

Waxing crescent

First quarter

Waxing gibbous

Full moon

Waning gibbous

Third quarter

Waning crescent

Third quarter
6

Waning crescent
7

5 Waning gibbous

North Pole

New Moon

4 Full moon

Earth's Rotation

1
Waxing crescent

3 Waxing gibbous

2
First quarter

26. The final illustration, with the phase images lined up, and the type positioned. The full moon is the enlargement.

the PICT file image looks like on top of the wire-framed sphere.

The only thing left to do before rendering the image is to point the light directly at the globe (23), and then we can render the final image of one of the phases (here, the almost half-full phase, the "waxing gibbous"). The ray trace tool (24) is used to render the image.

INTO FREEHAND

The images then are ready to be taken into FreeHand, where they're positioned and the type is set, and the full moon is enlarged (26). Also in FreeHand, an accompanying small graphic is drawn. It shows the relative positions of the moon phases (25). This graphic consists of downsized clones of the larger images. The final illustration is shown in Figure 26.

Down In Smoke

The Pathological Pit For Puffers

I took on a project for *Vim and Vigor*, a magazine for active senior citizens. The job was to illustrate a chart showing the relationship between cigarette smoking and heart attacks.

The magazine supplied a line chart (1). I felt that this chart really ought not to be a line, or "fever," chart, because these numbers don't show a trend over time. A bar chart would be more appropriate.

A bar chart compares the magnitudes of some variable—in this case, heart attack rates per 1000 men—as a function of another variable, such as levels of cigarette use. Whereas a fever chart shows time trends, a bar chart usually shows associations or correlations. It does not, however, portray causality.

The problem with having a solid line connecting the nodes of the different numerical values—the tops of the bars—is that such a chart may give the impression of simple, direct causality.

In the illustration at hand, it can be argued, forcefully, that the contribution of smoking to heart attack risk is now overwhelmingly established by the evidence. And, in fact, correlations are often portrayed with lines in medical and scientific journal articles.

CLIENT: *Vim & Vigor* magazine
TIME: 5 hours
SIZE: 90k
PROGRAM: Illustrator

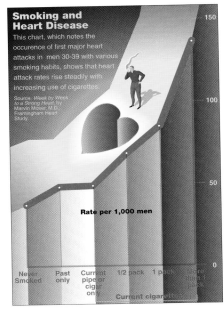

Smoking and Heart Disease
This chart, which notes the occurence of first major heart attacks in men 30-39 with various smoking habits, shows that heart attack rates rise steadily with increasing use of cigarettes.

Source: *Week by Week to a Strong Heart*, by Marvin Moser, M.D.; Framingham Heart Study

Rate per 1,000 men

Never Smoked · Past only · Current pipe or cigar only · 1/2 pack · 1 pack · More than 1 pack

Current cigarettes

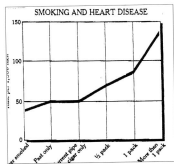

SMOKING AND HEART DISEASE

1. The client supplied this line chart.

However, there are countless situations in which charts are constructed in such a way as to imply causal relationships between two things when, in fact, there is at best an association or correlation.

The best advice is to be careful. Keep in mind that correlation is not causality. At any rate, I thought that in this case it was okay to keep the line, but I decided to make the chart seem more like a bar chart. Sort of a

hybrid between the two, at first glance, but a true bar chart.

DEVELOPING THE ILLUSTRATION

I tried out a bunch of different ideas for the illustration and did a lot of thumbnails. The four pencil sketches in Figure 2 were couriered to the client.

In the first thumbnail, cigarette smoke billows into a skull. The chart line would follow its side. Perhaps suitable for a running magazine, but not a magazine for older people. In the second, a smoker stands on a target, the smoke wafting upward along the chart line. Ho-hum.

In the third thumbnail, the smoker stands in a dangerous place, in the shadow of an ominous wall, which would be the chart. In the fourth, the chart line forms one side of the steep pathway, which has an almost unavoidable heart-shaped pit in the middle, with the smoker right above it.

In most of my chart illustrations the central image isn't formed around the chart line, but this was an exception. The client decided to go with this last conception.

Before starting the artwork, I sized the chart for its quarter-page slot, and put in the type. Next I took the chart line, traced it, and put it in the box, in order to see how much space the type would take up (3). Then it was time to draw a freeform path—the chart pathway.

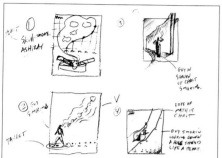

2. I submitted these 4 thumbnails. The fourth was chosen.

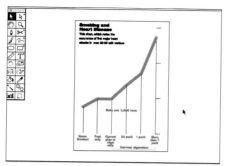

3. Before starting the artwork, I constructed the chart box and added the chart line and type.

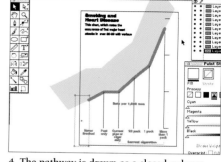

4. The pathway is drawn as a closed polygon.

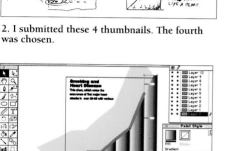

5. Gradient fills in the vertical polygons make the side of the chart look like a stylized cliff-side.

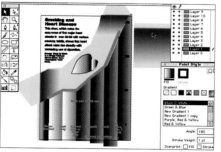

6. Gradient fills in the heart "pit" create the impression of an abyss.

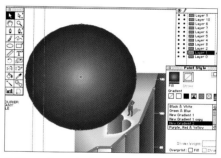

7. The pathway is also given gradient fills to lend it depth and shading.

8. The blend command creates the background glow above the pathway.

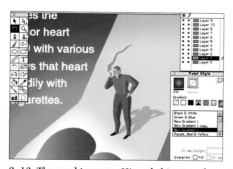

9, 10. The smoking man. His red shirt, together with the bright red of the chart line and the type, and the paler red of the heart pit, pull together the dominant color of the illustration.

I took the pen tool and drew the pathway, using the chartline as the lower boundary, and made it a closed polygon in Illustrator in order to fill it with a light yellow (4).

Into each of the polygons defined by the chart lines and the vertical lines from its nodes, I put a gradient fill (5). This created three-dimensional shading among these polygons, and also makes them seem rather like the bars on a bar chart.

I drew the heart "pit" on the pathway and also gave it gradient fills to create its abysmal appearance (6). I added gradient fills on the path-way itself to give it contour, highlight and shadow (7). The glow around the heart is created by making a copy of the heart shape, enlarging it, coloring it yellow, then blending it from white to yellow. The background glow above the pathway is also blended (8).

The Hassles of Hassayampa

Portraying Biohydrological Interactions

I live a good life as a home-based information illustrator. It's a good living, I'm my own boss, and I like what I do.

Most of the time, I get hired over the phone, I work entirely at home and don't visit the client, and the project goes smoothly. Then came the Hassayampa River, roaring down upon my neat little world.

The Nature Conservancy asked me to do a cross-sectional illustration of the Hassayampa River in Arizona—a diagram that would show not only its normally tiny channel but also its much bigger 10-year-flood channel.

The accompanying article would discuss the possibility that the floods do more good than harm, that the streamside forest ecosystems actually depend, for their continuing vitality, on the scrub-scouring action and the sediment-laying action of the flood.

This project was intensely demanding. The client had definite ideas and sometimes changing ideas about every detail. This sort of close monitoring is not unusual in projects involving technical diagrams, because objects and their interrelationships have to be rendered precisely and accurately.

It may be interesting to a reader

CLIENT: Nature Conservancy
TIME: 18 Hours
SIZE: 4,500k
PROGRAM: FreeHand

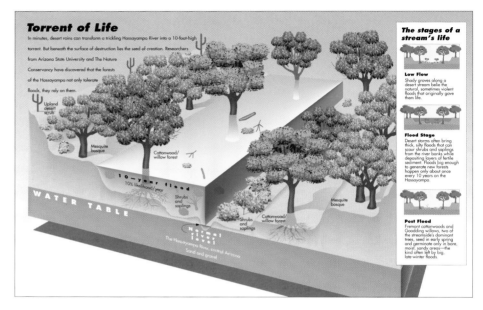

Torrent of Life

In minutes, desert rains can transform a trickling Hassayampa River into a 10-foot-high torrent. But beneath the surface of destruction lies the seed of creation. Researchers from Arizona State University and The Nature Conservancy have discovered that the forests of the Hassayampa not only tolerate floods, they rely on them.

Upland desert scrub

Mesquite bosque

Cottonwood/ willow forest

10—year flood
10% likelihood/year

WATER TABLE

Shrubs and saplings

Shrubs and saplings

Cottonwood/ willow forest

Mesquite bosque

The Hassayampa River, central Arizona
Sand and gravel

The stages of a stream's life

Low Flow
Shady groves along a desert stream belie the natural, sometimes violent floods that originally gave them life.

Flood Stage
Desert storms often bring thick, silty floods that can scour shrubs and saplings from the river banks while depositing layers of fertile sediment. Floods big enough to generate new forests happen only about once every 10 years on the Hassayampa.

Post Flood
Fremont cottonwoods and Goodding willows, two of the streamside's dominant trees, seed in early spring and germinate only in bare, moist, sandy areas—the kind often left by big, late-winter floods.

not experienced in the illustration business to see the progression of roughs, with their many notations and corrections.

The other interesting aspect of the illustration, from a technical point of view, involves the creation of the vegetation. There were about two dozen trees and bushes that all had to look similar but different.

DEVELOPING THE ILLUSTRATION

The Conservancy people wanted me to come up for a face-to-face work session, which I did, spending two hours there (a long time for a spoiled home-office type like me!)

The first reference material they gave me was a hydrologist's sketch of a cross-section of the Hassayampa River flood plain (1).

Based on this diagram I drew my first "rough-rough" with paper and pencil (2). This sketch, in which the cross-section is rotated about 40 degrees to give it depth, received a go-ahead and I went back home.

I set to work producing the first rough on the computer (3). Provisional text was positioned, contours were drawn, and the first positions of the trees and bushes are represented by filled ellipses and circles.

After I faxed this rough, the art director and the hydrologist indicated many corrections that had to be made. (They're jotted in pencil on the rough.)

The next day I faxed a second rough, with many changes made (4). The trees and bushes are starting to take shape, and the first images are drawn for the three sidebars. As happened with the first rough, I got back another round of corrections and changes to make.

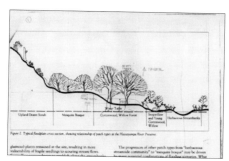

1. A hydrologist's cross-sectional sketch was the reference diagram.

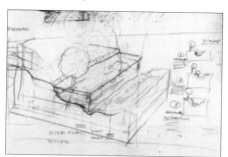

2. I drew this first "rough-rough" at the client's office.

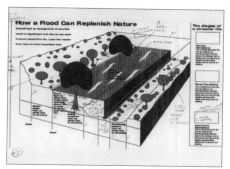

3. The first rough produced in FreeHand, with the first cut at contours and positions. Many changes had to be made.

4. The second rough, with still more corrections jotted in pencil.

A couple of days later I faxed a third rough, this one with the actual text in position and the right side of the floodplain added (5). Throughout these first three roughs, I added, deleted, and changed the positions of the trees, bushes, and shrubs (or their symbols).

These changes were difficult and complex to plan and lay out, but when I knew what I wanted to do, it was a manageable task to make the changes on the computer.

Using FreeHand, I could independently manipulate each object (such as a tree)—moving it, resizing it, changing its shape, or whatever—without having to redraw the whole illustration. The tremendous amount of time you save when you work with independently-editable objects is, to my mind, a compelling reason to trade your drawing board for a screen and a mouse.

After getting the third rough back with still more corrections to make, I produced a fourth, this time a tight, full-color print (6), which shortly boomeranged back to me with—guess what—more corrections to make.

Well, it finally happened that the changes were all made and a final image produced. The final typography, which I'd stored on another layer (8), was superimposed on the final artwork (7).

Figure 9 shows a close-up of some type. Each type element, such as "Cottonwood willow forest," is a

5. The third rough, with the right side of the floodplain added. The positions of trees and bushes have been changed, an easy matter in FreeHand.

6. The fourth rough, a tight color print.

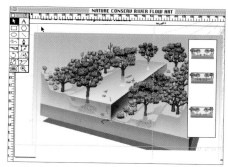

7. The final artwork, with perspective lines in the background.

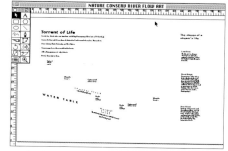

8. The final typography is set, ready to be placed onto the artwork.

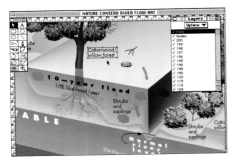

9. A close-up of type. "Cottonwood willow forest" is shown with its FreeHand "handles," which means it's been selected for some operation, such as repositioning or resizing.

10. This cloudlike shape served as a background for the leafy boughs I was about to construct.

11. I drew a bunch of ellipses of different sizes to represent leaves. These were rotated and/or skewed with the rotation and skewing tools.

12. One of the process colors for leaves, in the color palette I constructed for this illustration.

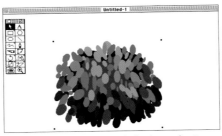

13. A completed bough, with the leaves having been put on top of the background.

14. I modified the basic bough to create various shapes.

separate object in FreeHand, so it can be moved around, rotated, resized, or otherwise manipulated.

CREATING THE TREES

The trees were constructed of clusters of individual "boughs," which were placed on trunk structures.

To build each bough, the first step was to make a cloud-like shape which would serve as the medium-to-dark green background to provide the illusion of deep leafy shadows inside a tree bough (10).

On top of the background shape, I placed a bunch of ellipses of different sizes, to represent leaves and leaf clusters (11). Then the ellipses were filled with different shades of green. An example is blue 100%/yellow 100%/black 80%, chosen from

the color palette I set up for this illustration (12).

The colored leaves were then put on top of the background shape, to complete the bough (13). The areas of the background which are overlapped by leaves are knocked out, both on the screen in FreeHand and in the printed piece

(Alternatively, you can choose the overprint option, in which overlapping inks print and transparent inks blend. Overprinting wasn't appropriate here, of course.)

When I had the first bough in hand, I cloned it and modified the clones, ending up with four basic boughs (14). I used these to build up all the trees, as well as the shrubs and the bushes.

The last step in building a tree was to place the boughs on the tree trunk and branches (16), which I'd drawn earlier (15). I placed different arrangements of boughs on each tree. The shrubs were also made of these boughs.

To make the different tree trunks, the basic trunk shape itself was cloned, and the trunk and branches were slightly modified so that they wouldn't all look the same. A close-up view of a typical tree is shown in Figure 17.

I drew the tree roots using the Wacom electronic tablet and a stylus (18, 19). This tool enables you to create very fine, delicately drawn lines, such as the ones you need to render the dendritic structures.

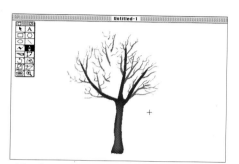

15. I drew a generic tree trunk and branches. It was easy to modify limb shapes and positions enough to differentiate the trees.

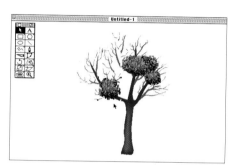

16. I put boughs on branches and moved them around, experimenting until I found a configuration that looked good.

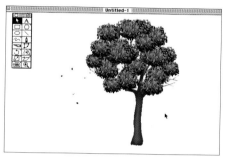

17. A typical finished tree.

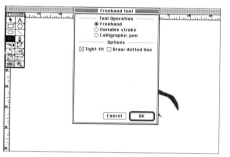

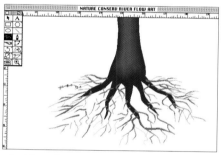

18, 19. The basic roots and their fine hairs were rendered with an electronic tablet and stylus.

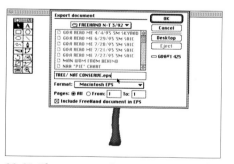

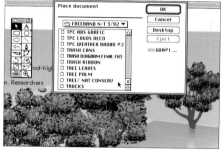

20, 21. The trees created massive memory drains and intolerable screen redrawing times. The solution was to save them as EPS files, then export them and place them back into FreeHand.

There were problems involved in drawing the trees, but there was another problem in storing them in the illustration file.

As I made more and more trees and bushes, I saw that they were gobbling up RAM. When you have a FreeHand file growing past a megabyte and not looking back, you've got trouble.

A very large FreeHand file redraws very slowly on your screen, and when you're in high gear, adding and changing things and then seeing what you've got, a bunch of two-minute or three-minute redraws kills a lot of time and slows your momentum.

One solution is to create massive-memory images as EPS (Encapsu-lated PostScript) files. This is what I did with the trees. I saved them as Macintosh EPS files (20), then exported them and placed them back into FreeHand (21).

An EPS image takes up far less memory, and requires much less redrawing time, than the same image drawn in FreeHand. (The reasons for this are quite technical.)

On the screen, the EPS image appears jaggier than it would if drawn in FreeHand, because it's a lower-resolution (72 dpi) file format. Not to worry, though: when you output your illustration to the printer, the EPS images are the same quality, the same resolution as the rest of the picture.

The Cost of Recycling

Trashin' and Cashin'

Popular Science magazine hired me to do a bar chart showing the cost, in dollars per ton, to recycle various waste products: plastic, aluminum, glass, cardboard, mixed paper, and newspaper.

The project was fairly simple and they pretty much left it up to me. I always like it when I'm free to let my creativity soar or, in this case, fester.

Repeat-clients tend to rely on your imagination and trust your judgment more than first-time clients, and this was the fourth or fifth time *Popular Science* had commissioned me. You can build up an "A-list" of regular clients by putting surprise into your graphics, and keeping it out of your deadline-meeting and invoicing. At any rate, that's what I always try to do.

The art director sent me a source table with the recycling cost numbers (1). He'd gotten it from the National Solid Wastes Management Association. Normally, as in this project, the client will supply you with whatever numbers you need in order to make a chart.

Occasionally, though, you'll be asked to do the research; or you'll do it because you're trying to pitch a project to a publication. Your local reference librarians are the place to start your search. If they can't direct

CLIENT: *Popular Science* magazine
TIME: 6 hours
SIZE: 360k
PROGRAM: FreeHand

you to a publication in the library that contains the information (see Chapter 5 of this book for some recommendations), ask them to look up the most likely trade association, or look it up yourself in the *Encyclopedia of Associations*.

A call to the trade group will often get you the numbers you need, or the name of the publication you need to look at—especially if you make it clear that your publication is going to call attention to them and to their subject.

DEVELOPING THE ILLUSTRATION

Since the numbers I'd be showing would compare different things

(commodities) with respect to a single measurement (cost per ton) at one point in time, I knew that a bar chart was the appropriate vehicle.

The next question was not so easy: What visual scene and symbols would most appropriately carry the bars, and most effectively grab the reader's attention?

I came up with two ideas, and did a "rough-rough" for each one. In the first conception (2), the bars are laid out horizontally, with icons representing the different recyclable commodities at left. At right a man would be emptying a box of trash into one of the bins of a material recycling truck.

The Cost of Recycling

	Unit cost (dollars per ton)
HDPE plastic	188
PET plastic	184
Aluminum cans	143
Amber glass	112
Green glass	87
Clear glass	73
Steel cans	68
Mixed-color glass	50
Corrugated cardboard	43
Mixed paper	37
Newspaper	34

"It was the obvious solution, which I finally bumped into, paddling around in the dark. "

The second idea (3) was to have vertical chart bars on top of a recycling truck, with symbolic icons at the tops of the bars. The client looked at this and said, "Oh, no, not another truck chart!" I guess they'd seen too many lately. But they did like the first idea. I turned on the Mac and palmed my mouse.

The first order of business was typing the commodity labels for the chart bars. Figure 4 shows the first seven labels entered in the FreeHand text entry box. With all the labels in place, I started constructing the chart bars (5).

I used FreeHand's rectangle tool (highlighted in Figure 5) to make the shapes, and the information bar—the line under the menu bar—to set the relative lengths of the bars. For example, the value "width: 143.2844" [points] in Figure 5 corresponds to aluminum's cost-per-ton figure of $143.

In like fashion I finished charting the bars, and put in their numerical values (6). Then, clicking on one after another with the shift key held down, I selected all the chart bars so that I could fill them with color as a group (7). Then I filled them all with a single keystroke (8)—ah, the feeling of power!

Some people are a little surprised that I use FreeHand to do my charting. They say, "Why don't you use so-and-so spreadsheet or charting program?" Well, the truth is that, except for very complex charts with

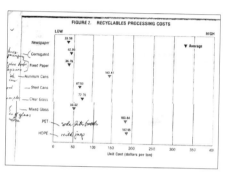

1. The source table was sent by the art director; he'd gotten it from a national trade association.

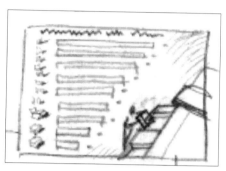

2. The first thumbnail conception had icons for the commodities at the left of the horizontal chart bars. With some modifications, this was the idea the client liked.

3. The client looked at this and said, "Oh, no, not another truck chart!"

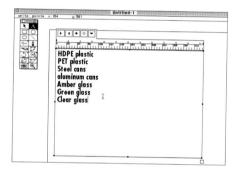

4. Having opened the FreeHand text box, I started typing the labels for the chart bars.

a great many values to plot, it's quick and easy to make charts in FreeHand—line charts, bar charts, pie charts, and hybrids or combinations of the three main types. Why waste time going into and then out of some other program, if there's no net time savings? You have to guard your time very jealously in the computer illustration business, if you want it to be profitable.

SWIPING A TRASH MAN
The next order of business was putting in the diagonal construction lines to guide me in drawing the recycling man and truck (8). Then I needed to draw a trash man—or find one. I sniffed around and found my man in a file for another project,

"Focus People Workin" (9).

I selected the man and his trash barrel and placed them in the current illustration (10). The recycling truck had to be drawn because I didn't have anything even close in my truck "swipe files."
I deleted the man's trash barrel because I wanted him to be unloading a box of trash paper instead. Then I drew the side of the recycling truck with its bins, and the curb (see the Final).

A SET OF ICONS
Now it was time to compile the set of small icons that would represent the different recycled commodities. I remembered that I had some

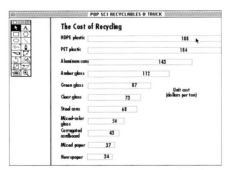

5. I used FreeHand's rectangle tool to make the chart bars.

plastic jugs and bottles in one of my image archive, or "swipe," files (11). I took them out of the box they were in and examined them (12). They looked re-usable (I'm a conscientious recycler, too).

Although Figure 11 shows the box covering the lower halves of the containers, I'd fully drawn them and put them one layer lower than the box's layer, so in fact each container was all there, electronically.

I ended up using two of these plastic bottles as glass bottles (there were four glass categories). The other two glass bottles I cribbed from another illustration for a near-beer ad (13). The final line-up of the icons for all the recyclable commodities is shown in Figure 15.

My first thought was to put the

6. This is a "good" set of numerical values for a bar chart: a lot of difference between high and low numbers, without extremes.

icons just to the left of the chart bars, and just to the right of the commodity labels (14). This didn't work. It didn't look right; the icons weren't drawing attention; the whole thing looked cluttered.

Then I got the idea to put a curb in the picture, angling diagonally behind the trash man (18). As I recall my train of thought at the time, as soon as I thought of the

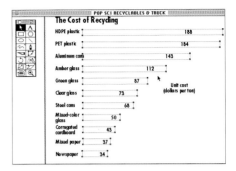

7. Next, I held the shift key down while I clicked on each bar, selecting them all.

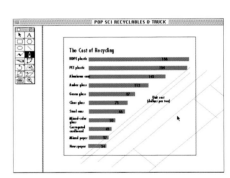

8. Selecting the bars as a group let me fill them all with a single keystroke.

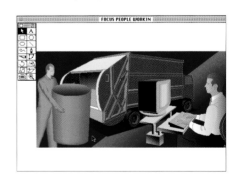

9. I recycled the trash man from an earlier illustration.

curb, I saw the icons standing out at the right of the bars, near the curb, waiting for the guy to come by and pick them up (16).

This left only one major problem: when I moved the icons to the right and the left edge of the bars next to the commodity labels, it became

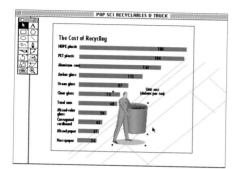

10. After placing him in the chart window, I removed the barrel.

11. I borrowed plastic jugs and bottles from another of my image archive files—"swipe files," I call them.

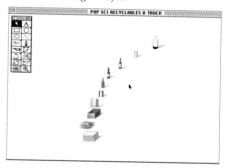

12. Each of the containers is all-there, electronically. The side of the box is a separate element on a higher layer.

13. I got the other two glass bottles from this illustration.

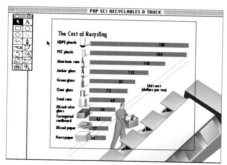

14. The idea of putting the icons between the type and the bars didn't work; it was too cluttered, and the icons didn't stand out.

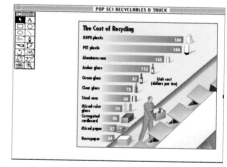

15. The icons on parade. Small symbols like these add interest to a great many of my illustrations, charts as well as diagrams.

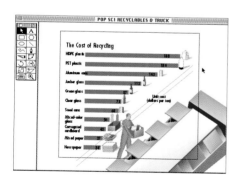

16. I had to find a way to cleanly separate the commodity labels from the bars.

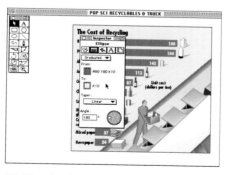

17, 18. I decided to put graduated, rather than flat, colors in the bars, changing from red on the right to the background color at the left.

apparent that a few of the labels would be right up against the bars, and one of them ("Aluminum cans") would end in the bar itself (16).

I couldn't move the left edges of the bars any more to the right without losing visual tightness. I couldn't figure out what to do, so I kept

working on other parts of the illustration. Finally I got the brainstorm: the chart bars wouldn't get flat color, but a graduation, starting with a saturated red at the right and fading out to the background color at the left (the process color settings are shown in Figure 17). This would allow "Aluminum cans" to plop over

in a completely unobtrusive way. It was the obvious solution, which I finally bumped into, paddling around in the dark. The final is shown as Figure 18.

Quakin' and Shakin'

Shear Madness at Fault

CLIENT: National Geographic	**SIZE:** 550k
TIME: 5 hours	**PROGRAM:** FreeHand

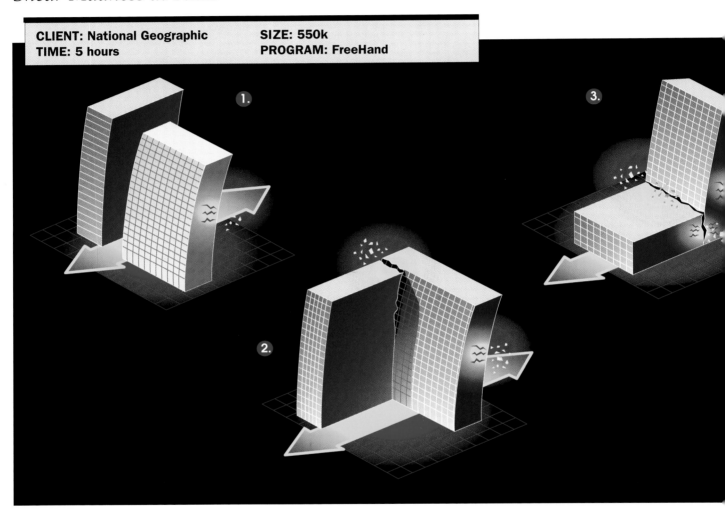

I was hired by the National Geographic Society's Book Division to do a set of illustrations showing how earthquakes stress-out and damage buildings. The images, a set of 6, were for the book *The Builders: Marvels of Engineering,* a compendium of articles on interesting buildings and structures.

The illustrations would necessarily be highly simplified, with few or no individualizing elements. The idea was to focus on a set of causal relationships: the effect of earthquake shear forces on various types of tall urban building configurations.

Basically, my approach was to design a few "generic" buildings, grids, and arrows which I then used, with different combinations and modifications, for all 6 images.

The final illustration is shown in Figure 1. It might be useful to discuss the conception as a whole, and then the "building blocks" of the images. First, the colors. The black background was well received by the editors, because it was going to be a common motif in many graphics throughout *The Builders.* I also preferred it, because it focuses attention on the buildings.

The rich primary colors used for the buildings and the earthquake effects contrast with the black, at the same time that the very emptiness of the black serves visually to further saturate the primary colors.

For comparison, look at the much less bold effect when the images are backed up by white (2). I developed the illustration in my mind. I

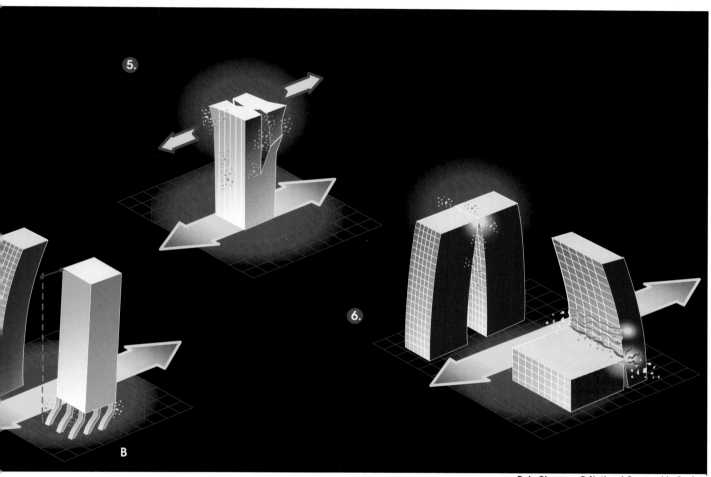

1. The final illustration, showing the 6 stylized building configurations rockin' to the Richter scale. The buildings, the arrows, the underlying grids—all were constructed out of a few "generic" forms.

saw the 6 stylized illustrations against the black background, and realized that I would need some kind of plane or platform to put the buildings on.

A solid ground-like surface would be the obvious choice, but I couldn't think of a color or texture for it that wouldn't diffuse the focus on the buildings. But a grid is always a good plane surface to put a scientific or technical drawing on. So the surface would be a transparent red grid against the black background. They would all be tilted about 35 degrees off horizontal, and the arrows (symbolizing the shearing forces of the slipping fault) and the buildings would be similarly rotated.

So I made one of the grids, with a round red "seismic force zone" in its center (3), and rotated it to the proper angle in FreeHand (4).

Then I cloned 5 more grids and positioned them. I made an arrow using two graduated fills (5) which I pasted inside the arrow outline (6). I cloned new arrows out of the first arrows as I needed them.

All the buildings were cannibalized from two originals. The building on the right in Figure 7 is a cloned, flipped, and modified offspring of the one on the left. Figures 8 and 9 show the buildings being moved into place and "joined." Figure 10 illustrates another clone and parent building.moved into place and "joined." Figure 10 illustrates another clone and parent building.

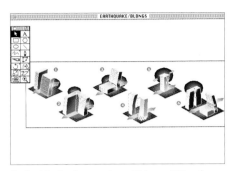

2. A white background would have diffused much of the visual focus that was achieved with the black.

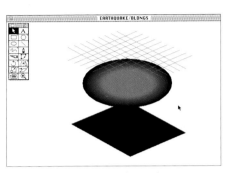

3. Each grid is made up of several constructions which are superimposed on the bottom rectangle.

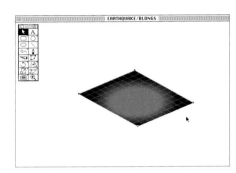

4. The grid lines and the red blend have been cut and pasted inside the rectangle.

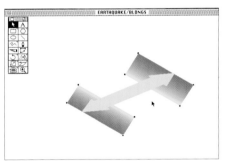

5. The basic arrow has two graduated fills.

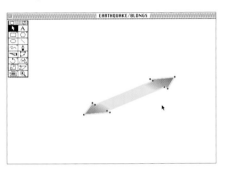

6. The fills are cut and pasted inside the arrow outline. New arrows are cloned out of this one as needed.

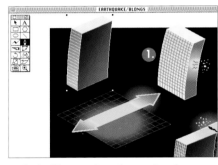

7. The building on the right is a cloned, flipped, differently colored, and curved offspring of the one on the left.

The important point to make about these grids, arrows, and buildings is that they were all quickly and easily generated in FreeHand out of just a few basic forms. This constitutes what might be called creative leverage. With state-of-the-art illustration software, you only have to invent the wheel once.

Speaking of not reinventing the wheel, it's worth noting that these buildings may well be re-used later in some other illustration.

I store many FreeHand images of common categories of objects such as buildings, people, cars and trucks, and animals. I keep them in what I think of as my personal archive files. For example, I have several files whose names begin with the keyword "Buildings." In these files are a number of images of

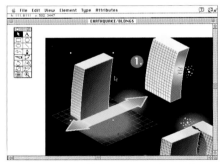

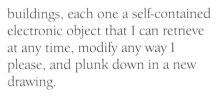

8, 9. The two buildings are moved into place and joined, now covering the arrow and red grid.

buildings, each one a self-contained electronic object that I can retrieve at any time, modify any way I please, and plunk down in a new drawing.

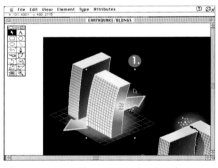

10. Another parent-child pair, the building on the right having been taken, with a few modifications, from the one on the left.

My People Files

Recycling Figures

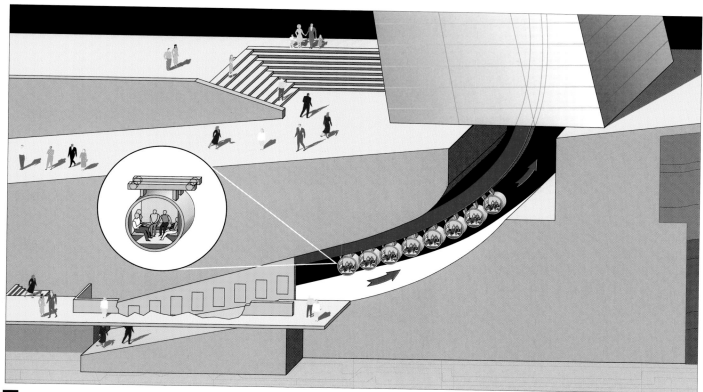

In some respects, computer illustrators are just like their drawing-table counterparts. For example, we all hate to re-invent the wheel.

When I need a picture, say, of a tree, a house, or a person, to use as a reference picture, I don't go to the library and start searching (unless the picture is of quite an esoteric or uncommon object).

Rather, I consult reference books like pictorial encyclopedias. Or I look through my personal image archives, my file drawers full of note

CLIENT: National Geographic
TIME: 7 hours
SIZE: 800k
PROGRAM: FreeHand

books, scrapbooks, and the like, where I store all sorts of images. (It goes without saying that neither I nor any of my peers resort to using commercial clip art!)

But often, when I need a drawing of an object that is more or less generic, I go to my Mac files where I store hundreds of stock images from my earlier work.

This demonstration will include a discussion of how I took people from previous illustrations and used them in a new graphic.

DEVELOPING THE ILLUSTRATION

I was doing some work for National Geographic's pictorial compendium of great engineering pro-

jects, *The Builders*. One of the illustrations would show a cutaway view of the internal curving tram train that carries passengers to the observation room at the top of the Gateway Arch in St. Louis.

The art director sent me an illustration of the newly completed arch; it had appeared in a 1965 *National Geographic* article (1).

This is nice work, but it had to be redone. The original artwork was gone and only a faded slide remained. Also, the painting, finely detailed and elegant, didn't fit the simplified, black-background style of the illustrations for *The Builders*.

I submitted a rough, on which the art director has written various corrections to be made (2). The rough incorporates my more stylized and less individualized rendering of the passengers of the capsules.

The contents of the eight tram cars, called "capsules," are all duplicates of one drawing, which is shown enlarged in the circular call-out at the left.

Using the FreeHand pen tool, I drew the capsule and its stylized passengers at 800%, then shrunk it down (3). One of the few frustrating aspects of using illustration software on the Mac is that it's hard to draw figures with fluid lines.

The best results are achieved at a high degree of magnification, say 400% or 800%, so that the figures are smoothed out somewhat when printed at 100%.

It was easy to make the eight capsules of the tram. I cloned the first one seven times, changing only the orientation of the mounting brackets that hold the capsules to the upward curving track (4).

ONE CHARACTER'S ODYSSEY

Whereas the figures in the capsules are "one-timers," which I used for just this illustration, many of the people in my drawings have had previous lives.

For example, look at the four people in Figure 5, which is a close-up of an above-ground area in the arch illustration. Let's trace the history of one of these persons, the third one from the left, wearing a dark suit.

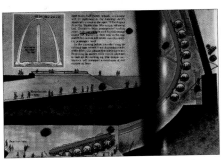

1. My reference illustration was a nice work done by Joseph Barrett for a 1965 *National Geographic* article.

2. My rough made the passengers more stylized. The figures in each of the 8 cars are identical.

3. The tram capsules and passengers. The people don't have features, because they'd have been too small to print legibly.

4. The interior of the first capsule is cloned 7 times to produce the 8 identical images.

He first appeared, in different garb, as a briefcase-carrying lawyer in another illustration (6).

I wanted to save him for possible future use, so I removed his suitcase, suit, and facial features (7). This made him a more generic figure, and also saved memory (it takes several hundred bytes to store a suit and probably several hundred more to store a suitcase).

In my group of Macintosh files whose names begin with the keyword "People," I store many, perhaps a hundred or more, of my stock characters, pulling them out to use again whenever I need them, and adding features, clothes, and accessories to fit the occasion (8).

Figure 9 shows the lawyer guy, along with all the other characters (including a bunch of square dancers) who inhabit the file "People Blue Collar."

It saves a lot of time to keep trees, cars, people, or other objects in personal archive files like this. Otherwise, if you wanted to use one of your "old" people in a new illustration, you would have to go searching through all your illustration files to find a suitable figure.

Not only would you probably not remember which file to go to, you'd also burn up time by waiting for each file to open—and for the program to redraw its images— so you could examine its contents. You can really kill a lot of time this way.

> **❝ It saves a lot of time to keep trees, cars, people, or other objects in your personal archive files. ❞**

5. Each of these people has appeared in one or more of my earlier drawings.

6. The suited gentleman got his start as a California lawyer.

7. To archive him for future re-use, I "genericized" him by removing features and clothes.

8. To store human figures for later use, I group together a bunch of files by beginning their names with the keyword "People."

9. Each person in the file is stored as a separate object in FreeHand. It can be plunked down in any project and edited as desired.

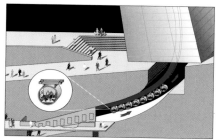

10. Most of the people in the final illustration were first created for other projects.

the question of which file has the image you want. There are at least two answers. First, you may not have a specific image in mind.

But if you've consistently and logically grouped files together under major categories (for example,

"People..." files), you can quickly go to one file after another and browse.

Second, you may have a particular image you want to bring up. The problem is locating it quickly. In Chapter 4 of this book, I discuss the matter of electronic image manage-

ment at some length. One of the points of that discussion is that some recently-introduced programs are powerful tools that you can use to organize, catalog, find, and retrieve your good old stuff.

Heart Balloon

Not Just a Bunch of Hot Air

In many assignments, the information I'm given to illustrate has an active quality. It might deal with a hurricane or a radio communications network or a cutaway view of the core of the sun.

In each case, the material portrays the dynamic relationships of things, processes, forces. It almost seems as if the information *wants* to be illustrated, so that it can jump off the page and visually hook the reader's interest.

And then there are statistics. Those bored-looking numbers trapped in the rows and columns of tables, or in the bars or pie slices of comatose charts.

As an illustrator it's my job to rescue these numbers and breathe new

CLIENT: *Vim & Vigor* Magazine
TIME: 6 hours
SIZE: 570k
PROGRAM: FreeHand

life into them, so that the reader will want to make their acquaintance, not look away.

I took on a project to chart "The Most Common Risks for Heart Disease." I'd be showing the 6 most common risk factors. The graphic presenting this breakdown would be one of the focal points in an article in a health and fitness magazine.

I needed to come up with an image that would call attention to these numbers—which, by their nature, are rather unattractive. First I came up with the image of the overweight, sedentary-looking juggler (1). This seemed to be a good way to

1. The first thumbnail, with the juggled hearts representing various risks.

symbolize the various risks, and suggest some relationship between them—but somehow I didn't think the image would be very interesting or attention-grabbing.

Then I got the idea of the heart balloon and sketched it (2). I considered how appropriate it was. At first glance, probably not as immediately "appropriate" as the juggled hearts. But riding a hot-air balloon is also risky. Especially a balloon that looked as if it were made of smooth taut mylar, inflated almost to the bursting point.

At any rate, I thought I could make it so visually interesting that people would stop and look. In a statistical illustration, any image that gets people to look at the information is appropriate.

DEVELOPING THE ILLUSTRATION

The development of this illustration involved techniques which pro-

2. But the heart balloon seemed a better attention-getter.

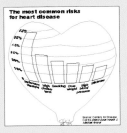

3. I drew the outline of the chart and the chart bars, and inserted the text.

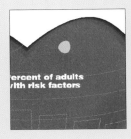

4. A highlight area is drawn and cloned. The clone is not visible, since it lies directly under the original.

5. The clone is enlarged and filled with a mid-tone.

6. A smooth transition from the highlight to the background is created by blending the two with the blend tool.

7. The corner of the gondola is blended.

> ## **"In a statistical illustration, any image that gets people to look at the information is appropriate."**

vide several good examples of the use of blends and graduated fills in Aldus FreeHand to create an airbrush quality.

After I drew the outline of the heart, I did the chart lines and text, and inserted them into the heart shape (3). In order to render the heart in an airbrush style, I had to properly place and blend the highlights and shadows. The highlights had to be on the two crests of the heart. After I rendered a highlight area (4), I created a clone—an exact duplicate of the highlight area—right on top of it. I enlarged the cloned shape and filled it with a mid-tone color (5).

The highlight is a light-tone, probably 10% red/10% yellow, and the mid-tone (the surrounding heart color) is 100% red/100% yellow. Then I blended the highlight into the mid-tone using the Blend command in FreeHand (6). I also used

the blend tool to produce the corner of the gondola (7).

To create the large tree at the bottom left, I first generated an ellipse to represent one of the stylized "branches" and blended the highlight area of light green to the darker green of the outer edge (8). Using the scaling tool, I duplicated several

of these curious melon-like objects in different sizes (9).

The one continuous-tone area that I didn't create with the blend tool was the sky. Here I used the graduated fill command, which is preferable to the blend command for showing color transition in an object with a regular shape (10).

8. The highlight and the darker outer shadowed area are blended to create the three-dimensional effect of the branch.

9. I duplicated the branch in different sizes, then stacked and restacked them until the treetop had the desired shape.

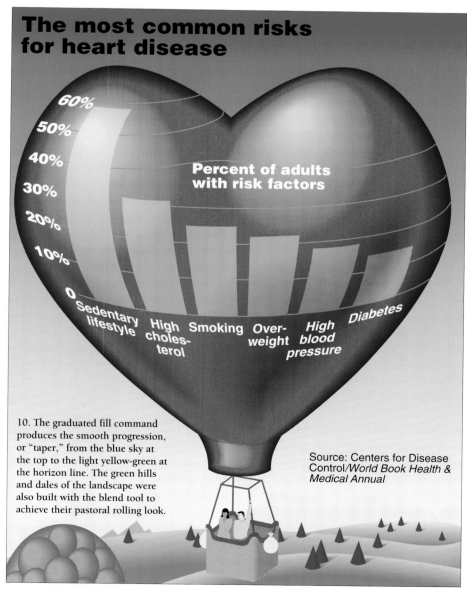

The most common risks for heart disease

60%
50%
40%
30%
20%
10%
0

Sedentary lifestyle High cholesterol Smoking Overweight High blood pressure Diabetes

Percent of adults with risk factors

10. The graduated fill command produces the smooth progression, or "taper," from the blue sky at the top to the light yellow-green at the horizon line. The green hills and dales of the landscape were also built with the blend tool to achieve their pastoral rolling look.

Source: Centers for Disease Control/*World Book Health & Medical Annual*

History of an Image

Glasgow Makes Big Strides

Oxford Health Plans, Inc. (OHP), a fast-growing regional health care company, hired me to do a set of 6 graphics for a marketing brochure directed toward prospective new client companies and their employees.

One of the illustrations would show the four major requirements that a physician must meet in order to qualify for membership in OHP's network of doctors. These requirements are listed in the memo they sent me (2). Notice that they refer to the criteria as "hurdles."

Yes, the client gave me the idea for this graphic. Their idea was that a figure representing a physician would be running over four high hurdles—the qualification criteria that the physician must meet.

It's actually fairly common for me to get the basic idea for an illustration from the client. It might be interesting to see how the hurdler idea went around.

HISTORY OF A HURDLER

I normally send a prospective client a set of my promotional sheets which contain samples of my work, going back five or six years. One of these "promo's" is shown as Figure 1. The client's decision to hire me is often, perhaps even usually, based on their reaction to the promo's.

CLIENT: Oxford Health Plans, Inc.
TIME: 5 hours
SIZE: 650k
PROGRAM: FreeHand

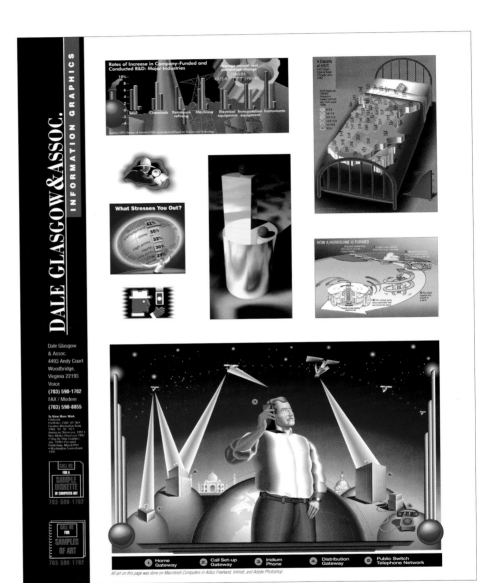

1. This is one of my self-promotion sheets. The client came up with the basic symbol for the illustration—a hurdler—from one of these.

The promo's aren't just sales tools, however. Often a client will get an idea from the samples. One of the illustrations will contain a symbol or scene that seems appropriate for the graphic he's hired me to draw.

As often as not, the things clients pick are from my more action-packed graphics, images filled with movement, energy systems, or natural forces. They seem to like these dynamic metaphors, which are a favorite motif of mine.

This happened with the hurdler. In one of my older promo's, the client noticed a bar chart dealing

> ## " It's actually fairly common for me to get the basic idea for an illustration from the client. "

with personal computer marketing channels (3). The chart was on a hurdle, and an executive carrying a PC was hurdling it. The client decided that the hurdling image was just right for the "credentialling graphic," as they referred to it. I more or less endorsed this view.

The computer-carrying executive wasn't the first hurdler, though. That graphic actually was based on an even earlier illustration.

Several years ago I was hired to do a chart showing various statistics about the incentive vacations earned by the employees of a meeting and convention planning organization, and I got a rather ornery image in my mind. The employees would be symbolized by a man running high hurdles, while chasing a carrot dangling from a stick which was tied to his head (4). (Fortunately, the people in this organization have a wonderful sense of humor.)

When I needed a hurdler for the PC retailing illustration, I took carrot-head out of his FreeHand file containing the image, put it in a new illustration file, and worked with it. First I flopped it, creating a mirror image with FreeHand's reflecting tool.

I took the carrot off his head and modified the torso, especially the arm positions, using the knife tool. And I added the PC, new hurdles, and a second hurdler following behind. So, while the final image (3) was mostly new art, having Mr. Carrot Head as raw material

2. Credentialling graphic
Idea: Physician type running high hurdles. each hurdle is a specific OHP network requirement.
Hurdles: Undergraduate pre-med training (optional)
Postgraduate residency or fellowship in accredited university program.
Board-certification within 5 years of graduation.
Ongoing Oxford Quality Assurance reviews.
Dale: Oxford's Quality Assurance Committee is a group of respected physicians, hospital administrators and other health care providers that reviews each physician's license, malpractice insurance, and professional references.

3. Client/Member/Physician retention chart
Idea: We're open to suggestions

2. The client sent the text information for the "credentialling graphic."

3. The client got the hurdler idea from the earlier illustration.

4. The hurdler originated as this carrot-chaser.

certainly saved time.Getting back to the OHP graphic, after I created the final color rough (5), I got back a color proof which the client had printed and then added corrections on a sheet of stencil paper (6). The final image is shown as Figure 7.

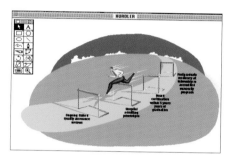

5. I submitted this color rough by modem . . .

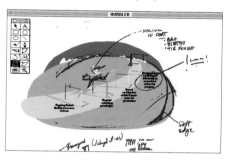

6. . . . and the client faxed it back with corrections.

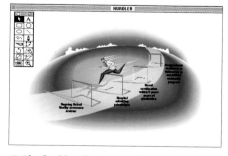

7. The final hurdler image. The landscape and sky have been softened and rounded with FreeHand blends.

125

The Structure of Castle Ramparts

Capturing the Crenelation of Caernarvon

I'm often hired to do a drawing which, from the outset, I know will not be exciting or technically interesting. This happens a lot when the assignment is simply to render an object.

In a project for *The Builders*, National Geographic's pictorial encyclopedia of engineering masterpieces, I was assigned to diagram the inner and outer structure of a typical tower rampart at Caernarvon Castle in Wales.

The information I was going to show was both architectural and functional: castle tower ramparts, at least Caernarvon's, were not built to be romantic backdrops for chivalric movies about knights and fair ladies.

Every aspect of their construction was designed to help achieve their fundamental purpose: to enable defenders to keep all invaders from climbing the walls.

As important as the information I would show was the information I would not show.

Not to be shown were things like weathered surfaces, irregularities, holes where chunks had fallen out or had been removed, mosses, weeds, different-colored building stones, dirt and stains, bird droppings, and all those other things that add charm to ruins.

CLIENT: National Geographic
TIME: 4.25 hours
SIZE: 300k
PROGRAM: FreeHand

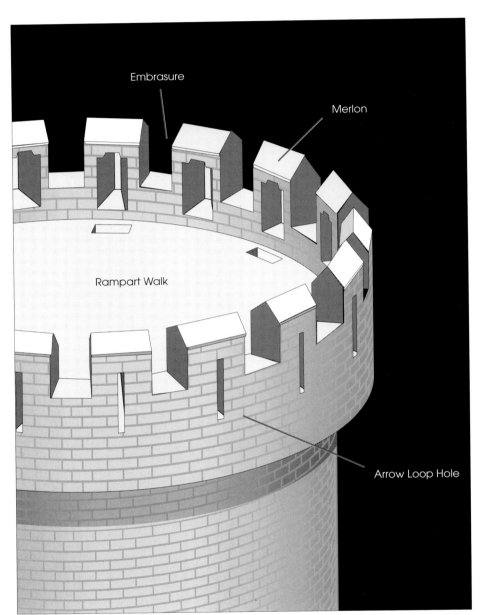

Embrasure

Merlon

Rampart Walk

Arrow Loop Hole

Dale Glasgow © National Geographic Society

The illustration, to show the ramparts' structure cleanly and simply, would have to leave out a lot of the things which make photographs of Caernarvon Castle so singularly striking.

This would allow me to concen-trate on the important things, like crenelations, machicolations, embrasures, and merlons (these words aren't just for spelling bees).

I would try to do a clear and concise rendering of something which can't adequately be portrayed

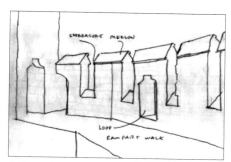

1. The reference diagram was useful but was too different from the book's style of illustration to use as a model.

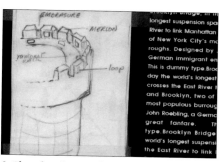

2. The other drawing that the art director sent was used as a model: it had the desired graphic simplicity.

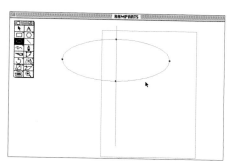

3. This ellipse was generated to set the plane of perspective.

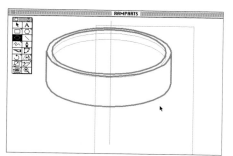

4. The basic tubular structure of the battlement was founded on 3 ellipses. The second and third were cloned from the first.

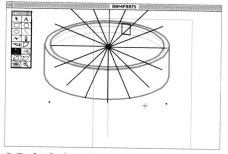

5. To divide the wall into sections, so that the notches, or "embrasures," could be drawn, I used the rotating tool.

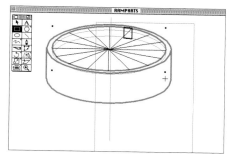

6. Next I drew the boxes. . .

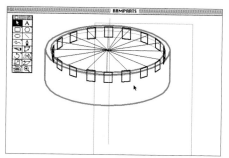

7. . . .which would define the solid areas of the wall, the "merlons."

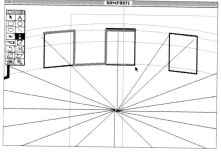

8. Using the pen tool, it was quick work to draw lines connecting the boxes.

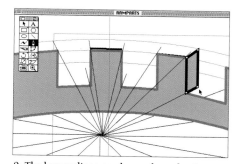

9. The box outlines are dropped out, leaving a solid inside wall which is filled with grey. One of the side walls is drawn.

through photographs or words. That's enough of a reason for an art director to commission an illustration, and for me to do it.

DEVELOPING THE ILLUSTRATION

For each of the illustrations in *The Builders,* the editorial staff at

National Geographic found or prepared reference sketches or photographs for the illustrator.

They sent me a reference diagram done by the art director (1). This was useful, but too detailed and different in style from the format of the other illustrations in the book.

The art director also supplied me with a rough pencil drawing (2), which, because of its graphic simplicity, I chose to use as the model for the illustration.

My first task was to get the vantage point or plane of perspective. I did this by making an ellipse that

127

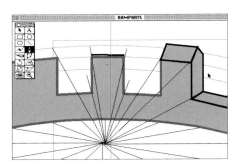

10. The pointed top and other planes are drawn. Temporary construction lines have been added to guide perspective.

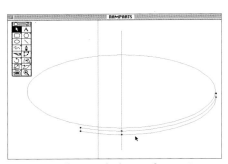

11. To start drawing the layers of stone, I brought up the original ellipse again and cloned part of it twice, to form the top and bottom lines of a stone row.

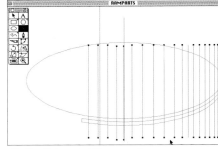

12. Parallel vertical lines cut the two arcs to mark the borders between individual stones.

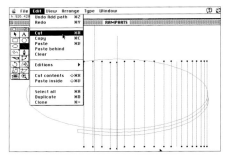

13, 14. After cutting and pasting the vertical line segments into the curved polygon, I had the first row of stonework.

would represent a circle lying on a plane which was inclined at an apparent 40 degree angle to the page (3). I drew this on an outline of the illustration box sized to specs.

I wanted to render the basic shape of the battlement as a tube structure. To do this I cloned two more ellipses out of the first, and the same shape as the first, using the wonderful clone tool (4).

One represented an outline of the inside of the wall, and the other delineated the floor of the rampart. (The bottom ellipse was cut in half with the knife tool, and the top half was discarded.)

Next I divided the wall into sections, so that the solid portions of the wall, the "merlons," and the rectangular notches in the wall, the "embrasures," could be drawn. Since there were to be 16 equal sections in the wall, each section would be 22.5 degrees of the ellipse. Using the rotating tool, I quickly marked off the sections. First I drew one line out from the center of the ellipse, cloned it, and rotated the cloned line 22.5 degrees. Then I power-

duplicated this sequence of commands 15 times to finish marking off the sections (5).

Using the scaling tool, I fit the section lines into the inner ellipse. Then I drew the box shape for the first merlon (6), and the rest of the boxes (7). Each box was positioned so that its upper right corner was at the point where one of the construction lines hit the inner ellipse.

I drew lines connecting the box shapes, which, except for the pointed tops of the merlons, outlined the solid portion of the wall (8). After placing more construction lines to set perspective, the base of the side wall of one of the embrasures is drawn with the pen tool (9).

The pointed top of the side wall is extended from the base, and then the other planes are drawn (10). The rest of the notched wall is finished in this manner.

STONEWALLING

Let's turn now to another problem, that posed by the question of how to render the layers of stonework on the outer wall of the rampart.

Once again, we start with an ellipse. Then we draw two arcs by cloning part of the ellipse and use them to represent the thickness of one row of stonework (11).

To mark off the lengths of individual stones, I drew vertical lines. There was no math to this; I used

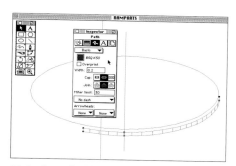

15. I colorized it black 50%/blue 10%.

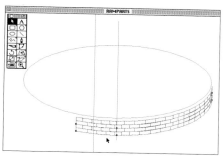

16. After the second row is created by cloning the first, these two are cloned and pulled down, resulting in four.

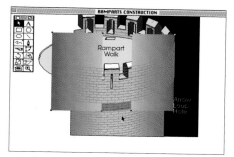

17. These are two of the graduated fill blocks which render the transition from highlight to shadows on the sides of the rampart.

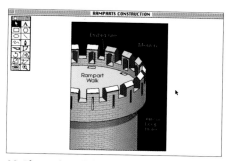

18. The graduated fills have been pasted inside the stone pattern.

visual feel to shorten the lengths as they arced around the side of the castle tower (12).

Then I cut off the tops and bottoms of the vertical lines (13), leaving only the short segments inside the curved polygon representing the top and bottom of the row of stonework. After executing the "paste inside" command, I had the first row of stonework (14), which I then colorized a blue-black (15).

The second row of stonework would have to be offset to the alignment of the first, so it had to be cloned off the first row, pulled down under it, and moved laterally. Then the first two rows are cloned, and

pulled down to create two more rows (16). Then this sequence of actions (clone, pull down) is power-duplicated, which quickly creates the rest of the rows of stonework. FreeHand, which wears many hats, here was quite willing to be my stonemason.

After the rows of stone have been drawn, they need to receive highlights and shadows in order to render their rounded look. This is done through graduated fills.

Two of the fill blocks are shown in Figure 17. They were set up to produce a transition from the midtone grey at the center of the rampart to the darker grey at the sides.

"FreeHand, which wears many hats, here was quite willing to be my stonemason."

After the fill blocks are positioned, they're cut and pasted inside the stonework pattern (18). That's pretty much it. Other aspects, most prominently the front and back views of the tapered arrow loop holes, also had to be drawn.

But basically the illustration was a straightforward, solid if unexciting, exercise in FreeHand, using its basic tools in all sorts of different ways to do a complex job. Just as a car mechanic relies on his wrenches, screwdrivers, pliers, and measuring instruments, so an illustrator relies on his pen and rotation tools, clone and cut and paste commands, and graduated fill operations.

Both toolboxes help put bread on the supper table.

Getting A Leg Up

More Posturing by Glasgow

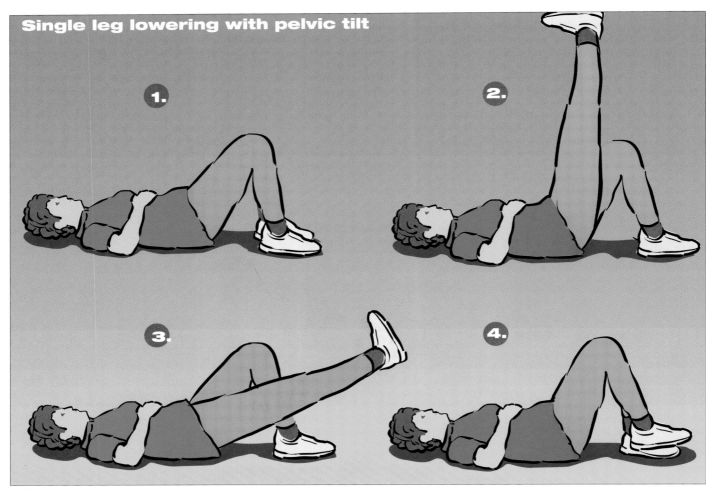

Single leg lowering with pelvic tilt

1.
2.
3.
4.

Sometimes I get hired to do a series illustration. In this type of diagram, there are usually two graphic elements: (a) a stable, anchoring image or part of an image that does not change, or only changes in minor ways; and (b) variations which show the progression of steps or changes from the start to the finish of a sequence of actions. *Prevention* magazine was preparing

an article, "Super Six—Best Bone Exercises for Busy Days," which would present a routine of exercises to help strengthen bones and prevent osteoporosis.

They needed diagrams which would show how to do each exercise. Each illustration would have to portray, in a very simple way, the successive positions that a person would go through to do the exercise properly and safely.

In this lesson we'll look at how I constructed the four sequential

images for one of the exercises. Basically, I created one illustration—the woman reclining with her left leg bent at the knee and the foot stationary on the floor—and manipulated the right leg and foot through the four positions in the sequence.

DEVELOPING THE ILLUSTRATION

The client sent four photographs showing the exercise positions (1). I scanned them and placed them into a new FreeHand file. Having put the scans on a lower foreground layer, I started tracing the first image (the

CLIENT: *Prevention* magazine
TIME: 5 hours
SIZE: 170k
PROGRAM: FreeHand

top photo in Figure 1) in the current drawing layer. As Figure 2 shows, tracing over a scan (at any rate, a low-resolution scan like my present scanner yields) is not an exact art.

I used the photo as a guide, in combination with my knowledge of the human face and figure. For reference, I mounted the actual Polaroid photo in front of my handy adjustable magnifying glass (3).

The few points I placed in my tracing of the woman's arm, for example (4), were enough to outline a FreeHand path over the arm

I then defined the curves between points by manipulating the electronic "curve handles" which the program attaches to each point.

FreeHand uses three types of points to define its "paths," the freeform line segments in graphics that are rendered with the program.

A *curve point* creates curves between two adjacent points. A *corner point* creates an angled change of line direction. A *connector point* makes transitions between straight and curved line segments.

After I quickly traced the outlines of the various parts of the body (5), it was time to switch from the pen tool to the freehand tool, so that I could apply "brush-and-ink" strokes to loosen up the lines.

FreeHand's "freehand" tool is used to draw continuous freeform lines and shapes. In this instance,

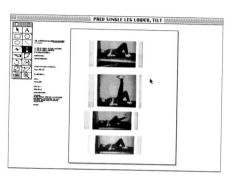

1. These photographs by Ansel Adams were supplied as references. I scanned them in.

3. For easy reference to fine details, I had the actual Polaroid mounted in front of my adjustable magnifying glass.

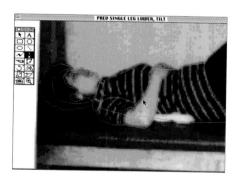

5. The quickly-traced outlines of the various parts of the body. The next step is to apply broad "brush strokes" over these lines, using FreeHand's "freehand" tool and an electronic tablet and stylus.

I've chosen the dialog box settings (6) to let me render broad strokes with the Wacom electronic stylus and tablet. I choose the thickest stroke, 2 points.

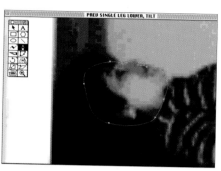

2. I traced part of the photo at a time, zooming in to a 400% magnification for greater accuracy and control.

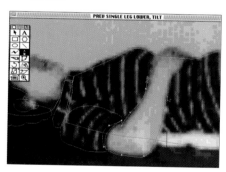

4. As the close-up of the woman's arm shows, you need only to place a few points to outline a shape in FreeHand. For fine tuning, you can adjust the "handles" (not shown) for any point.

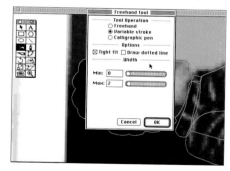

6. So that I would be able to render broad brush-strokes with the electronic tablet and stylus, I set the maximum stroke width at 2 points.

First, I dropped out the scanned TIFF image to a background layer—I didn't need it any more at the moment. Only my tracing lines were then left on a lower foreground layer.

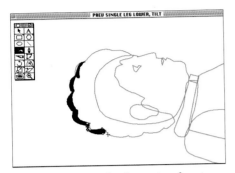

7. After positioning the electronic stylus at a point on the woman's hair, I started making very loose brush strokes.

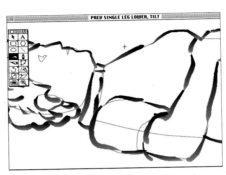

8. A close-up of the "brush-and-ink" strokes done with the Wacom stylus reveals the looseness of the style.

9. In order to get her color palette, I copied the woman in another exercise illustration and pasted her into the present graphic.

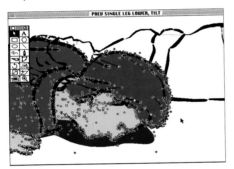

10. After I pasted in the woman, I discarded her. I just wanted her for her palette. Electronic exploitation at its worst.

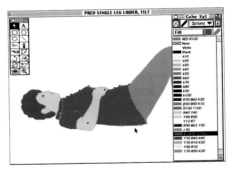

11. A close-up of the blue shirt, with the color palette at the right. The color is blue 100%.

12. The final image of the first exercise position. The shadow has been drawn on an underlying layer.

On the highest foreground layer, the current drawing layer, I positioned the stylus at the appropriate place on the tablet, at a point on the outline of the woman's hair.

I started applying the "brush strokes" in a very loose sort of style which simulated the brush-and-ink technique (7). At the beginning of the stroke I got a thicker line by pressing down on the stylus, letting it taper at the end of the stroke by easing up on the pressure.

As the close-up in Figure 8 shows, this was very unlike the tight, fine-lined, precise drawings that I usually do. The loose style was appropriate for these drawings because they're really glorified stick figures. Their only function is to show the different exercise positions.

Since the brush strokes are actually shapes, rather than lines (8), I'm able to give them graduated color fills. You can tell FreeHand, via its "styles" palette, to apply any type of fill you desire—flat color, graduated color, patterns, etc.—to multiple elements in an illustration. In this case, the elements are the contents of the layer containing the brush strokes.

I wanted to use the same colors as I did in the previous exercise diagram, "Modified Push-Up" (9). So I copied the woman in the earlier graphic, and pasted her into the present illustration document—it didn't matter where (10). The idea was to crib her "color palette" for the present illustration.

When you bring in an element (an image or part of an image) from another file, whether a FreeHand file or a file from another image-manipulation program using the PostScript language, FreeHand automatically brings along the color palette, the set of specified colors that was used in rendering that element.

Figure 11 shows a close-up of the woman's blue shirt, and the color palette at right. The process color, highlighted on the palette, is blue 100%. Figure 12 shows the final

13. For the second exercise position, the right leg is raised at a 90 degree angle to the trunk.

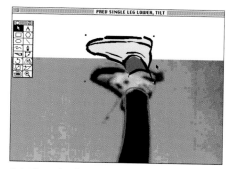

14. The right shoe is selected for copying.

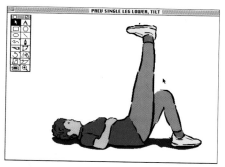

15. Then it's rotated and moved to the top of the raised leg.

16. Using the rotating tool, the vertically-raised leg of the second position is lowered . . .

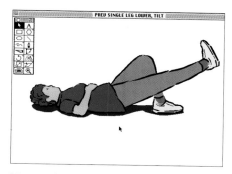

17. . . .to the barely-raised position of the third position.

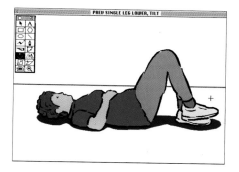

18. To get the fourth position, the bent leg of the first position is selected for manipulation, then rotated slightly to lift the right leg a bit.

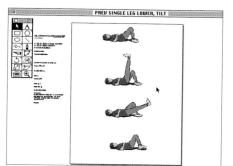

19. The final illustration with the four exercise positions.

image of the woman in the first exercise position. I've drawn a shadow, which I've put under her by putting it on a lower layer.

POSITIONS 2, 3, AND 4

In the second exercise position, the right leg is raised at a 90 degree angle to the trunk (13). As I did in constructing the first image, I traced over the photo for the second position (1), then drew the brush strokes with the electronic stylus, and filled the outlines with the same colors as the first image.

To save the few minutes it would take to trace the shoe again, I copied the shoe from the first image (14), rotated it, and moved it to the top of the raised leg (15).

Creating the third image was a simple matter of lowering the vertical leg in the second image. The leg is selected as an element so that it can be manipulated independently of the rest of the body; then it's low-ered into position with FreeHand's rotating tool (16, 17).

The slightly-raised leg position in the fourth image is similarly constructed by rotating the bent leg of the first image (18). The final illustration is shown in Figure 19.

After all is said and done, these were throwaway drawings, ephemeral, loosely rendered, quickly executed, and soon forgotten—but, I hope, helpful to *Prevention* readers who wish to strengthen their bones.

Humble Pie

Enough is as Good as a Feast

In a nutshell, the main goal of an information illustrator is to graphically communicate information—facts, relationships, processes, trends, or what have you—in a clear and engaging way.

Sometimes you have almost too much information to show in one graphic, and it's a challenge to keep the info-bits clear and distinct. This was the major task I faced in "Canadian Cartographic Chit-Chat," for example, which is analyzed elsewhere in this chapter (p. 54). That graphic, I think, does its job well enough, communicating a lot of information without seeming too "packed."

On the other side of the spectrum are those assignments in which you have only a few bits of information to present. In statistical illustrations, these often take the form of what I call the "single-breakdown chart."

This type of chart takes a single topic, such as "income" or "high blood pressure," and breaks it down by some characteristic, such as "income source" or "cause of hypertension."

The breakdown is usually a percentage distribution.

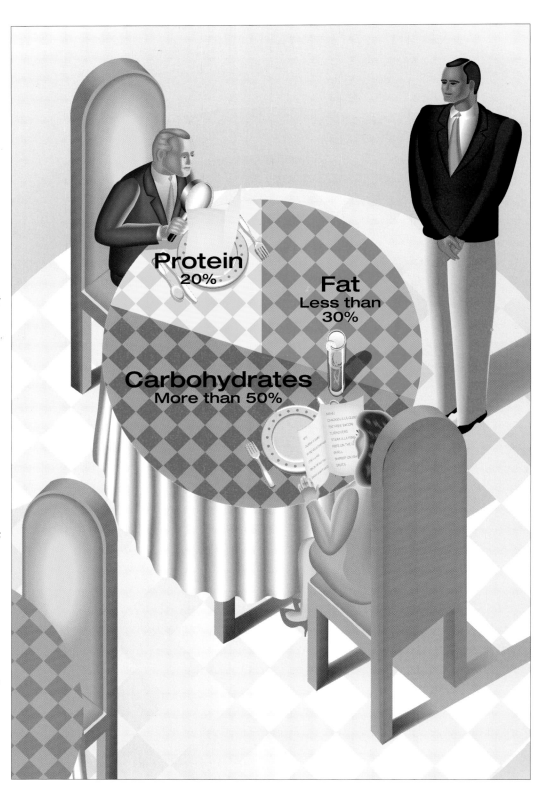

There may be as few as two numbers to be shown, and rarely are there more than eight or nine.

I like to do illustrations for single-breakdown charts because of the special challenge they pose: there are only a few statistics to show, yet they must be communicated in a way that gets the reader not only to stop and look, but also to keep the numbers in mind, as they read.

You could almost have a "law" which says, "The fewer the numbers in a statistical illustration, the more important each number is for the communication."

Second Wind, a magazine for active seniors, asked me to illustrate a three-number breakdown: the recommended dietary division of calories from fat (30%), protein (20%), and carbohydrates (50%).

The article explored the problems of trying to find restaurant meals that conformed to, or even approached, these guidelines.

DEVELOPING THE ILLUSTRATION

The client had decided on a table as the central symbol, and sent me a sketch (1). The chart in the sketch is what is called a "fever chart." It is primarily used to show trends over time, and is inappropriate for a percentage breakdown.

A pie chart was called for, and I decided that the round tabletop was the vehicle for it. I did a couple of thumbnails (2), then a final color

1. The client supplied this sketch—a "fever" chart, inappropriate for showing percentage breakdowns. A pie chart was called for.

2. I did these thumbnails.

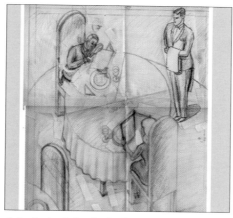

3. I submitted this final color rough, which was approved. The magnifying glass was meant to symbolize the careful scrutiny with which the dieting diners are reading the menu.

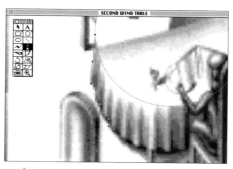

4. After scanning in the rough, I traced the outline of the tablecloth.

rough that was approved (3). It would be a simple yet elegant design, one that would give center stage to the three numbers.

From a technical point of view, there are two interesting constructions in the table: the tablecloth folds, and the segmenting of the tabletop to show the three statistical percentages.

After scanning in the final rough, I started tracing the outline of the tablecloth, using the Freehand pen tool (4). Then I traced the individual folds, separating them into sections, and deliberately extending the tops and bottoms so that they would overlap the tabletop and the shadow on the floor (5). Later this excess would be cut out, resulting in the perfect abutment of the shapes.

To create the shadows and highlights of the folds, and thus the illusion of depth, I outlined a highlight "sliver" in the center of each section, then made each section a closed polygon, ready to be blended with FreeHand's blend command . The blended sections, with the transitional tones between highlights and shadows, are shown in Figure 7.

After removing the construction lines which defined the closed polygons of the sections, the next step was to cut off the jagged edges at the tops and bottoms of the tablecloth sections.

First I had to get the outline of the tablecloth folds that I had done earlier and stored on a lower layer in

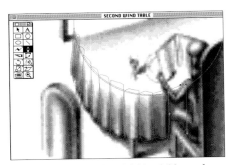

5. I traced the individual folds, deliberately extending the tops and bottoms so they would overlap the tabletop and the shadow on the floor.

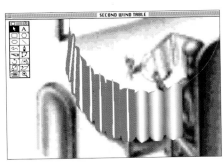

6. I made each fold section a closed polygon and drew the highlight "sliver" in the middle of each one.

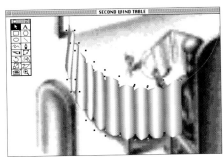

7. The blended sections, showing the transitions from highlights to shadows.

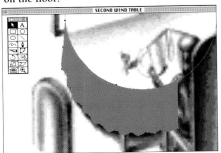

8. The tablecloth outline which I had traced earlier (Fig. 4) now is used as the clipping path to cut off the excess tops and bottoms of the fold sections.

9. The cut-out shape is pasted inside the outline.

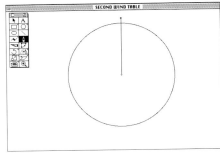

10. The protractor is started by drawing a circle and a line into its center.

FreeHand. I used this outline as an electronic cookie cutter (or "clipping path," in FreeHand terminology) to cut off the excess tops and bottoms of the sections (8).

All that remained was to paste the cut-out shape inside the outline (9).

Another technically interesting aspect of the table involves the sectioning of the tabletop into three sections, corresponding to the 30% fat, 20% protein, 50% carbohydrate division of the pie chart.

In order to accurately mark off the three angles, you need to construct a protractor which divides a circle into 100 equal slices, each having an arc of 3.6 degrees.

Many spreadsheet programs have

charting capabilities; you can produce a protractor and then import it into FreeHand. I use spreadsheets to construct complex charts, but, always looking for the most efficient way to do things, I found that you can most quickly make a protractor using FreeHand.

First, you draw a circle using the ellipse tool (you get a perfect circle by holding the Shift key down as you drag the mouse).

You extend a line into the center of the circle (10), then clone the line and rotate it 3.6 degrees, using the rotating tool (11). This tool rotates an "element"—in this case a line—around a fixed point (the center of the circle). This rotation generates the first 3.6 degree slice, which is 1

percent of the circle.

After this it was an easy job to generate successive additional slices by pressing the Duplicate command. This command copies, or "power-duplicates," the last sequence of transformations—the initial 3.6 degree rotation—using the same fixed point and settings.

Keeping the trigger finger on this command, the circle is very quickly sliced up into the 100 equal sections (12), and presto, you have a usable protractor.

To define the 3 pie slices to represent the 30%/20%/50% breakdown of the data, I counted off 30 slices (the dietary fat recommendation) and drew 2 lines to mark off the sec-

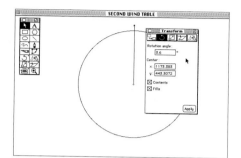

11. I've told FreeHand to rotate the line 3.6 degrees (clockwise) to create a one-hundredth-part section of the circle.

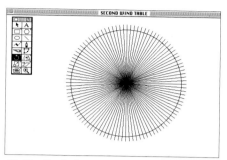

12. The finished protractor: the circle divided into 100 equal slices—each to represent a percent.

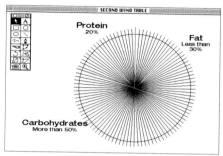

13. I drew the heavier lines to mark off the 30%/20%/50% sections.

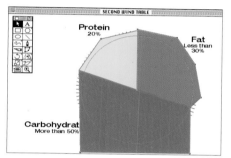

14. I made 3 closed polygons over the sections and filled them with colors.

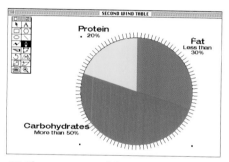

15. The excess parts of the polygons are cut, and the fills are pasted inside their pie slices.

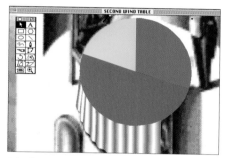

16. The pie chart is positioned to be the tabletop.

tion and make it a fillable closed path in FreeHand. Similarly, I marked off the 20% for protein, leaving the 50% carbohydrate section (13).

To fill the 3 sections with colors, I drew 3 polygons and filled them with colors (14). Then I cut and pasted the color fills so that they precisely fit their sections (15).

After cutting off the protractor lines that extended outside the rim of the circle, the pie was ready to assume its role as the tabletop (16). The final illustration is shown at right as Figure 17.

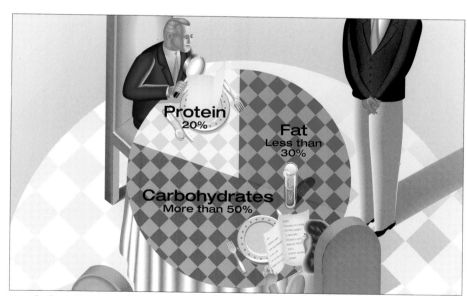

17. The final illustration. Certainly the most elegant pie chart I've ever drawn.

CLIENT: Second Wind
TIME: 6 hours

SIZE: 1,200k
PROGRAM: FreeHand

Pixel-Based Proto-Galactic Renderir

Trust Me . . .

Most of my illustrations are drawn in FreeHand or Illustrator. These and other illustration programs are called "object-oriented," because they allow you to build graphics consisting of mathematically described "objects," which may be shapes, lines, colors, fills, type, or other illustration elements.

Most important, the objects can be resized or trans-

formed without loss of resolution, and an object or group of them may be changed independently, without affecting the rest of the image. This means that you can experiment all you want, moving things around, stacking parts of the illustration on layers, and changing the stacking order of layers.

This is all well and good—the ideal type of program for

CLIENT: Illustration for Glasgow & Associates ad
TIME: 2 hours
SIZE: 594k
PROGRAM: Photoshop

PIXEL-BASED PROGRAMS

Pixels, the display dots on a computer screen, are the tiny electronic "grains" that all images are composed of. You might say that the pixels are gridlocked: there's a fixed number of them, each with a specified location on a grid; they don't move around; they're locked in place.

In a pixel-based program, everything you do is on one layer, the grid of pixels. You apply colors, textures, lines, filter effects or other distortions, text—all on this layer. That's the limitation, the tradeoff for the program's continuous tone-rendering capabilities. You can't move things around and stack and restack elements easily (although there are ways to do masking, using "alpha channels" or similar features). What you *can* do is achieve the very fine, subtle, elegant effects of continuous tone art like airbrushing and watercolor.

One of the best pixel-based programs is Adobe Photoshop, a powerful image enhancement and manipulation program. Photoshop works well with other graphics programs (see "One Image, Three Programs," p. 99). It also works with most graphics file formats, including TIFF, PICT, EPS, Amiga, and Targa.

Photoshop's many features include:

1) A large set of digital filters and other tools for editing images and creating special effects.

2) Sophisticated color correction controls and color creation palettes.

3) Airbrush, paintbrush, pencil, and other painting tools.

4) Animation capabilities.

Photoshop is not just a place to process images, howev-

doing the kind of illustrations I do most often: tight, precise ones with well-defined shapes.

But sometimes you want to be looser. You want to do continuous-tone images, with their fuzzy fringes, irregular dithers, blurs, fades, glows, sprays, clouds, asymmetries, even "imperfections." For doing images like these, you're better off using a pixel-based program.

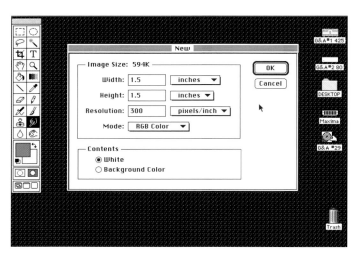

1. The image size will be 1.5 inches square. The resolution is set at 300 dpi (here, "pixels/inch"), which conforms to the rule of making your image resolution twice that of the printing resolution (150 dpi). 300 was also a high enough resolution so that individual stars, 1 pixel in diameter, would be visible but not "pixelized."

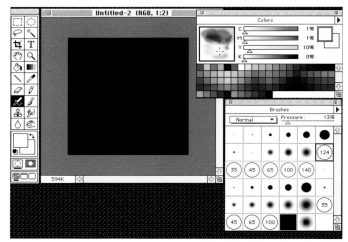

2. The new illustration workspace in Photoshop. The tool palette is at left. The blank illustration window is right of the tool palette. In the bottom right is the airbrush grid. The color palette is at the top right, with its three features: mixing well, color bars and sliders, and color grid.

er. You can create original illustrations or fine art images in this program that are extremely laborious or impossible to render in one of the illustration programs. In this discussion we'll look at the creation of an original image in Photoshop.

I've been working on a number of space illustrations for a visual dictionary. One of the diagrams is a three-image sequence showing the three main stages in the formation of a spiral galaxy. The first image shows the too-dense cloud of gas that is just beginning to condense into a bright disk, from which the stars in the spiral arms, and the blindingly bright nucleus, will later form. We won't reconstruct the picture that appears in the dictionary, but a new image which I am planning to use in an ad.

DEVELOPING THE ILLUSTRATION

The art director sent eight or ten reference illustrations: various artistic conceptions of galaxy formation, as well as pictures of presumably analogous phenomena such as the formation of individual stars.

These illustrations all visualized someone's very educated guess as to what a forming galaxy looks like; there were no photographs. Even if photos of proto-galaxies existed, the editors had a prohibition from using scans of photographs as the basis for any image in the dictionary .

So, although I assimilated various impressions from these pictures, I was pretty much on my own. I ended up basing my image more on the art director's textual description than on any of the reference illustrations.

I didn't do any pencil thumbnails or roughs for this drawing. If I had done any preliminaries on paper, they probably would have been in pastels. Given the fineness and smoothness of the textures in the illustration, and the extremely subtle color gradations it would require, I knew it made the most sense to start work directly on the Macintosh, creating an original image in Photoshop.

SETTING RESOLUTION

First I created a new document file in Photoshop and set the image size: 1.5 inches square (1). Then I had to pick the resolution. It had to be set high enough so that the very small dots representing single stars in the forming galaxy would be visible, but not look oddly rectangular, or "pixelized."

At 150 dots per inch (dpi)—the resolution at which the image would be printed—a star represented by a single pixel (as most would be) would be clearly visible, but would appear pixelized. At 300 dpi, the white dot would be barely visible, but not have a perceivable shape. Also, the gas clouds I'd be drawing would look slightly granular

> **These diffuse, soft-edged pixel sprays can't really be duplicated in an object-oriented illustration program.**

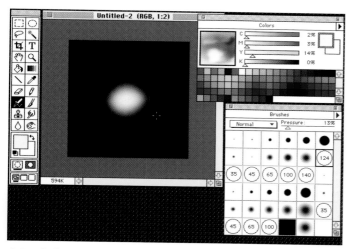

3. For the background glow, I start laying down a white pixel spray with the airbrush—which is actually the Wacom electronic stylus applied to its tablet.

4. Photoshop's airbrush tool is more efficient than a real airbrush because it lays down color (here, the white glow) faster. With a traditional airbrush, you have to keep spraying over and over. Photoshop's electronic paint colorizes pixels once and that's it.

at 150 dpi, but smooth as cotton candy at 300.

These considerations suggested a resolution of 300 dpi, a conclusion which was reinforced when I thought of the general rule for printing electronic images: the resolution of the art the illustrator supplies should be twice that of the printed image, which was going to be 150 dpi. So 300 was the lucky number (1).

THE COLOR PALETTE

Then it was time to confront the blank screen, the black empty space of the new illustration window (2). I selected the airbrush tool (highlighted on the tool palette on the left in Figure 2) and opened the Photoshop color palette: the rectangle in the upper right part of Figure 2. (Photoshop has another color selection feature, the "color picker," which is more powerful and more complicated, but we won't be using it here.)

You can use the palette in three different ways and switch instantly from one way to another.

First, you can choose a color from the standard color grid—the five rows of cubes at the bottom, which also has space for custom colors you create. Or, using the brush and smudge tools, you can mix your own colors on the square "well" box above the grid. Using the mouse to

position the crosshair, select a color from any spot on this mixing area, and click. (Photoshop calculates the color composition percentages for any spot you select.)

Finally, you can adjust the sliders on the color bars above the grid and to the right of the mixing well. You can use any of three models (and, of course, switch at will from one to another): HSB (hue, saturation, brightness); RGB (red, green, blue); or CMYK (the cyan, magenta, yellow, and black process colors). When you're not manually adjusting the color bars, they show the composition of the color you currently have selected in either the mixing well or the grid.

Don't worry, you can only select one thing at a time, so it will be clear what the percentages refer to. In Figure 2, the color bars show the composition of the color selected on the mixing well, at the center of the crosshair: 1% cyan, 1% magenta, 10% yellow, and 0% black.

AIRBRUSHING THE RINGS

Finally I'm ready to start laying down color on the blank screen. I take a fairly large airbrush—124 pixels in diameter—and spray a white glow in the center of the image (3). This glowing area will perfuse light through the interstitial spaces of the bands of gas clouds I'll airbrush over it, making it seem as if there is an inner core of ener-

5, 6. The glowing central area no longer dominates. As I keep spraying, variously applying pinks, reds, yellows, and browns, the rings take on more depth and color interest.

7. Auras are added above and below the "surface" of the evolving gigantic disk of gas clouds. They're airbrushed also, of course.

gy, heat, and light.

I select a smaller airbrush tip and start hand-drawing the vaguely elliptical rings of cosmic gas clouds around and over the glowing central area (4, 5, 6, 7). The first bands are shown in Figure 4.

These diffuse, soft-edged pixel sprays can't be duplicated in an object-oriented illustration program like FreeHand, which can produce perfect elliptical shapes, or let you render deliberately "imperfect" ones—but always shapes with hard edges. Even to approximate the ethereal effects in Figures 4-7 would require a lot of time-consuming and memory-eating blends.

Figures 5, 6, and 7, works in progress, show the progressive deepening of the bands as I continue to "spray" by hand and eye. (Keep in mind that this airbrushing is done with the electronic tablet and stylus.)

What happens if I get slack with the airbrush and make some skewy, out-of-proportion lines? Do I have to trash the evolving image and start over? No. You just black out an area you don't like and spray right over it (believe me, this happened many times).

PIXELS OF THE FIRST MAGNITUDE

With all the gas cloud bands having been laid down with the airbrush, I turn to the matter of sprinkling individual stars throughout the bands. Opening the brush options dialog box, I select 1 pixel as the diameter, and "999%" as the spacing (8). I'm not sure what "999%" means, but the practical effect of choosing it is to make the airbrush (as it's manifested by the Wacom electronic stylus) apply the single pixels intermittently, with regular spacing between them.

This feature enables me to make continuous sweeping movements, in line with the elliptical swirls of the bands, while, at intervals, single pixels are whitened to make the individual stars. It's a lot quicker and much less vexing than it would be to manually place each little white spot.

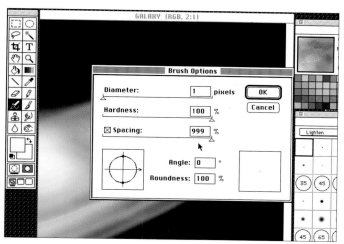

8. The brush options dialog box settings for the job of rendering individual stars, 1 pixel in diameter.

10. The final image. This isn't, incidentally, the picture that appears in the dictionary. For reasons related to the need for cosmogonic accuracy, the illustration above had to be redone (at this writing I'm still working on it).

The close-up in Figure 9 shows the stardust on the left side of the proto-galaxy. The final rendering is shown in Figure 10. (Final for this book—I keep re-doing it!)

RAM REQUIREMENTS

Before closing this discussion, we should take a moment to consider the hardware demands a high-end painting program like Photoshop places on your system. In order to fully take advantage of the program's speed, power, subtlety, and finesse, you need a high-resolution color monitor, preferably with a screen size of 15 inches

9. Stardust. By setting the spacing at "999" you tell the airbrush—the electronic stylus—to apply a star: that is, to colorize a single pixel white—at intervals. This lets your continue your sweeping motion, instead of having to stop and apply dots one at a time.

or more, and you need as much RAM as you can get.

Photoshop requires slightly over five megabytes of RAM just to run the program—not including any images you work on, and your images will probably run anywhere from 300-400k to several megabytes (the image we're currently reconstructing takes up 594k, and it's a comparatively small one). You'll probably want at least 20-30 megabytes of RAM even to think about serious hot-rodding.

(This recommended minimum also applies to most of the other illustration and drawing programs we discuss in this book. My system in its present setup has 32 megabytes of RAM, but I dearly would like to have 100 meg's or more. Unfortunately, buying multiple-meg's of RAM is still an expensive proposition, as a browse of the advertisements in *MacUser* will attest. I discuss the RAM-requirement in a little more depth in Chapter 2 of this book.)

The Health Security Card

On Assignment for the White House

For our last discussion in this chapter, we'll look at the development of what is certainly the most important illustration I've done so far.

On September 22, 1993, President Clinton presented the outline of his landmark health reform plan to Congress and the nation. At one point in the speech he displayed a prototype of his proposed Health Security card, which every American would get and which would be irrevocable.

I designed the card.

To be chosen for this assignment was very flattering, and it was quite satisfying to pull it off. No cakewalk, by any means, but a unique experience for an information illustrator. I'll tell you as much about the interesting aspects as I prudently can.

THE SELECTION PROCESS

The White House Office of Communications called the managing editor of *USA Today* and asked him to recommend several D.C. area illustrators for the job of designing the graphic materials for the Clintons' health care reform package: the pamphlet explaining the plan, which would be widely distributed among the public; and the national Health Security card.

The *USA Today* managing editor of graphics and photography, Richard Curtis (by happy coincidence, my old boss), named several other illustrators and me as potential candidates.

I was contacted by the Communications Office and asked to submit samples of my work. I did so immediately, sending all of the dozen or so self-promotion ads I'd sent out over the last several years. They called and asked me to come up to meet them.

I visited the Communications Office in the elegant Old Executive Office Building next to the White House. It felt great to walk

CLIENT: The White House
TIME: 36 Hours
SIZE: 1.300k
PROGRAM: FreeHand; Photoshop

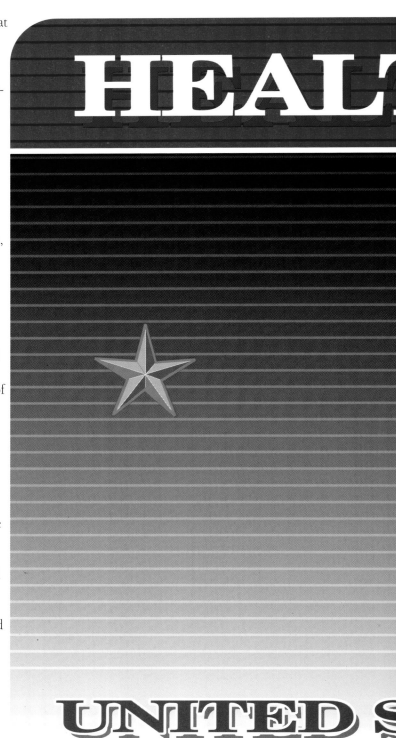

"At first I thought, well, I'll do up a set of nice tight pencil roughs and submit them. But after I'd done a few I realized that if I really wanted this job—and I did—it was essential that I go all out, prepare finished illustrations on the computer, and have them printed in full color. I think it got me the job."

up the steps and go in, on official business. My wife Sharon and I met with four people: Meeghan Prunty, Assistant Director of Research in the White House Office of Communications; Bob Boorstin, Director of the Office of Communications; and White House staffer Christine Heenan and advisor Dr. John Silva.

They were very nice, complimenting my work, and were especially interested in some of the illustrations I'd done in the area of health care. One example was the set of images I drew for an Oxford Health Plans, Inc., booklet; this job is discussed elsewhere in this chapter (see "History of an Image," p. 124).

The meeting seemed to go well. My hosts were impressed by my experience in health care-related illustrations, by the ads I'd sent, and, I hope, by me.

This was on a Friday. They asked whether I could put together some sketches to illustrate the main topics they had in mind for the pamphlet—by Monday morning. I said yes. Famous last words. I drove home and threw myself at the task.

DOING WHAT YOU HAVE TO DO

At first I thought, well, I'll do up a set of nice tight pencil roughs and submit them. But after I'd done a few I realized that if I really wanted this job—and I did—it was essential that I go all out, prepare finished illustrations on the computer, and have them printed in full color: all by Monday morning. Sometimes, in retrospect, I find that I've spent too much time and effort on an initial presentation. On the other hand, the more polished and profes-

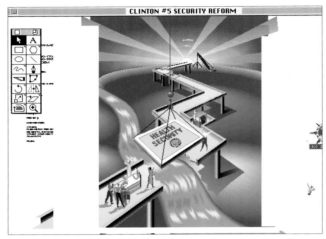

1. Before I started working on the card, I was drawing illustrations for the explanatory pamphlet. This image symbolizes the crooked, obstacle-filled road to health security . . .

2. . . . which will be repaired by the Health Security card.

sional your presentation is, the more likely you are to get the job. I don't like the regret that says, "If I'd only put in a little more effort . . ."

The first decision I had to make was the choice of the overall graphic theme for the pamphlet. After I read and reread the first draft of text for the pamphlet, I chose roads as the main motif: winding roads, crooked roads, roads with dead ends, a fork in the road, crossroads. They would be natural symbols for the twists, turns, and obstacles which confront the average American family in its quest for secure health care.

By Sunday afternoon I was working on the final renderings in FreeHand on the Mac. Figures 1 and 2 show one of the five illustrations I sent by modem to the service bureau on Monday morning and had printed on a 3M color printer.

A crooked elevated highway, symbolizing the difficult road to health care security, has been washed out by the torrent, creating one of the gaps Americans have in their health insurance coverage. The text discusses problem areas such as the loss of coverage many people encounter when they change jobs, or the inability of many small businesses to afford to carry health insurance for their employees. The washout will be repaired by the "Health Security" section being lowered by the crane. The section represents both the proposed program and the health security card.

These images (and the others) have undergone various changes since this version, and may be revised yet again

Set 1. The first set of card designs was knocked out from 7-10 a.m., working in FreeHand on my Macintosh IIx. Although these were first cuts, several of their elements stayed and formed the basis for subsequent designs: "Health Security" at the top, in the dignified New Century Schoolbook style; graduated color in the background; stars; horizontal stripes; and a central symbol. The caduceus made an early exit.

  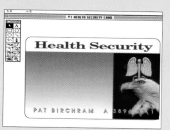 

3. The first version has as its central symbol an eagle which I found in an old book on engraving, scanned, opened as a FreeHand file, and traced and fixed up. The motto, which I made up, was canned.

4. I quickly rejected the sans serif style of the first card: it lacked the necessary dignity. Although I used the Helvetica again in several later versions (7, 8), the White House staffers agreed with my choice of New Century Schoolbook.

5. This eagle came from one of my image libraries on CD-ROM.

6. The layouts of this and the preceding design were inspired by the big open spaces on many credit cards. The trouble was, this card wasn't supposed to look like a VISA.

Set 2. The versions in this set have "United States of America" at the bottom (why I left it out of the first set I'll never know.) Several variations of colors and lines are tried, and the eagle has built its aerie in the center of the emblem—for now. It was thought that the eagle (or whatever the final symbol might be) would be a hologram. This notion was later dropped.

7. The eagle has been temporarily chosen as the central symbol, and "United States of America" has properly been added at the bottom.

8. This and 7 are the last mock-ups with sans serif type.

9. Serif arrives on the scene.

7.   8.   9.

before the pamphlet is finished. (You'll understand that I can't show you the current, near-final illustrations for the pamphlet before the President shows it to the press.)

Anyway, on a Friday afternoon in July, while I was doing the illustrations for the pamphlet, Bob Boorstin said that it was time to start working on the health security card; the President and First Lady wanted to see it. Could I sketch out a few ideas for our midday meeting on Monday? No restrictions; I'd have carte blanche.

Yes, I said. Several other projects demanded my immediate attention, so I first had to finish them over the weekend. Then, on Sunday evening, with my slate clean, I started thinking about ideas for the card. I must confess that I felt somewhat insecure—what qualifications did I have for producing a card that would be in every American's wallet? Besides, I'd never designed a plastic card before.

A STUDIO OF CARDS

Nevertheless, on Monday I sat down at the terminal at 7 a.m., looked at the thumbnails I'd sketched on Sunday, and started cranking. During the next three hours I produced the first four card designs and ran them out on my laser printer. Then a long black limo came and drove me back to the Old Executive Office Building (just kidding).

This first set of cards (3-6) had several basic elements: the title "Health Security," graduated color in the background, stars, parallel lines for visual relief, a central symbol, and a motto (which I made up). I was trying for a clean, clear, uncluttered, and authoritative design. It had to have the weight of the U.S. Government behind it.

Set 3. In the third set, the Great Seal begins to compete with the eagle for the central symbol position. I scanned it into Photoshop and softened it up with filters and warm colors. Although some subsequent versions had the eagle, the totally authoritative Great Seal ultimately shot it down.

10. The eagle's last aerie.

11. This was my favorite design. I felt the elements were particularly balanced and harmonious in this one. The Great Seal is tried as the central symbol in the emblem.

12. The first card with "Health Security" in all caps. Otherwise it's a very unsuccessful version.

The first card (3) has an eagle as the symbol. I found the model for it in an old book on engraving. The second card has a medical symbol, the caduceus (4), and the third and fourth have these symbols unbordered and placed on the right side (5, 6).

Bob Boorstein was happy to see these designs; they had the sort of look he felt the Clintons would like: dignified, official, uncluttered. These first four were only a starting point, but it's easier and more productive to brainstorm when you have some solid ideas off which to bounce new ones. This afternoon was the first in a series of productive and exciting sessions.

There were a couple of conclusions from this initial set: the eagle was preferred to the caduceus, and the serif style, New Century Schoolbook, had the dignity that the sans serif Helvetica New lacked.

In my second set of designs (7-9), the circular eagle emblem is the central symbol. "United States of America" is now at the bottom (how on earth did I manage to leave that out?) The two main type elements are now in their permanent positions.

Different colors, white space, and pinstripe positions are tried in these three designs; but still more versions—many of them—remain to be rendered and evaluated.

On to set number three, then sets four, five, six, and seven. I knew that I had a lot of patience and resilience—

essential traits for an information illustrator—but the depths of my reserves surprised me on this project.

VARIATIONS ON A THEME BY GLASGOW

In the third set (10-12), the eagle is still used as the central symbol in one version (10), but now the White House people have asked me to put in the Great Seal of the United States. I did so, finding the Seal in a reference book, scanning it, and livening up the colors and contrast in Photoshop (see description below, "Seal of Approval").

Figure 11 shows the design that was my favorite among all the versions I produced. I liked the red, white, and blue composition: red type over white, the graduated blue fading out behind the red "United States of America," and the more pronounced grey stripes. Unfortunately, it didn't pass muster.

Neither did the next one (12), with the blue and pink elements and the thick dark border around the emblem. (It did happen to be the first card with "Health Security" in all caps, which resurfaced in the final card.)

I did eight versions for the fourth iteration (ahem!) of cards (13-20), and sent them in via courier. All the versions had a white background behind the upper/lower case "Health Security," and varied in just about every other respect except the two stars. I felt we were getting close to deciding on a final version, and I wanted to include every reasonably promising variation of colors, type, central symbol, and emblem border.

Some of the card versions in this and other sets—for example, the one with the pink background in Figure 17—look a little funky to me now; but they did serve the purpose, perhaps, of defining the extremes.

A CHOICE IS MADE

The four versions in set 5 (21-24) were produced by me on the spot at the Executive Office Building. I took along my high-capacity disks and drives with the illustration files, and did the new cards on one of the in-house Macs. We all sat around and brainstormed changes, and I implemented them. They were new wrinkles on the basic design developed in set 4.

I liked the design shown in Figure 21. This particular background made it seem regal and authoritative, in an American sort of way. Like the others in this and the following set, it has drop-shadow type. Lukewarm approval. Let's do another. The next one (22) is blue-dominated in a sort of Diners' Club style. This one was considered boring; not enough color, no red.

Then there was my "gold card" (23). I thought this one had the solid, secure, comforting look of something that was backed by the U.S. Treasury. The consensus was that this one, like the preceding one, didn't have red. It was time for some serious redness.

I reversed "Health Security" and put saturated red behind it. "That's it!" was the unanimous response (24). It wasn't my favorite, though. The colors are a little heavy, with no visual "rest area." Nevertheless, it probably is the most color-filled of all the designs. It was shown to various key people in the White House, and evidently they all agreed that this would be the design of the card the President would hold up.

COLOR PROOFS

So the verdict was in; the winning design was chosen—sort of. The staffers wanted to see a few more variations of the rest of the card coupled with the red bar at the top. Also, I wanted to do a few more versions because I wanted to get some Cromalin proofs. I wanted to see what the

Set 4. The eight versions of the fourth iteration. I did them at home and couriered them up to Pennsylvania Avenue. It seemed that we were getting close, so I felt it was time to present a real mulligan stew of variations in colors, borders, type, and symbols. They served two purposes: helping us decide what we didn't want, as well as what we did.

13. The first of the "big eight." They all had a white background behind the upper/lower case "Health Security," but varied in most other respects.

14,15. Reds & blues & blues & reds. . . .

16. Along with 20, the only version without the two stars which symbolize freedom. Get them out of here.

17-20. Versions like these help me set color constraints and limits because they elicit unanimous rejection. There's a risk in putting in duds, though—sometimes a client likes them.

different blues and reds would look like on a printed card. What you see on a color monitor may or may not look the same, or even close.

The final reason for doing a sixth set (25-31) was that the idea of having a hologram surfaced again. The original idea of using the Great Seal for a hologram symbol had been rejected. Now someone came up with the idea of putting in another symbol that would print under the embossed name and Social Security number of the cardholder. So I put in a waving flag beneath the Great Seal emblem in the versions of set 6.

But the hologram idea was again canned. The consensus was that it was too glitzy; and the security reason for it—that it would make it almost impossible to make counterfeit cards—seemed to have lost force, perhaps because of the fact that everybody would have a card anyway. Whatever the reason, the waving flag was run back down the flagpole and furled.

So I did a last bunch of cards, mainly varying the blue background for color checks, even including one (31) with a solid blue without gradation. My service bureau did a rush job on the Cromalins and sent them back.

The colors were true for the chosen card design. The final art for the card the President displayed on September 22, 1993 is shown in Figure 32.

As for the back of the card, we did about ten versions. The final is shown in Figure 33. The dark bar at the top is

Set 5. I did these cards at the Executive Office Building on one of their Macs. We brainstormed the conception for each one, then I rendered it quickly on the spot. My favorite was number 23, but 24, with its solid red bar at the top, won the prize. It's probably the most color-heavy of all the designs.

21. The fourth set was the decision set. I hoped this one would be picked; it wasn't. All designs in this and later sets have drop-shadow type.

22. More of a primarily monochromatic, credit card style. Not enough red.

23. The "gold card." I thought this one would really appeal to the public. The gold has the backing of the U.S. Treasury.

24. But this one won the cigar. It was the saturated red bar behind "Health Security" that everyone liked, I guess because of the way it counterpointed the blue. With minor changes, this was the card the President held up in his September 22, 1993 speech.

the magnetic strip. (All I had to do then was find a credit card manufacturing company and get them to make the small run of sample cards. That, of course, is another story.)

SEAL OF APPROVAL

Although the basic layout and all the versions were done in FreeHand, one critical operation was rendered in Adobe Photoshop: the softening of the Great Seal, which is the symbol in the central emblem of the card.

When I found a reproduction of the Great Seal and magnified it (34), I was immediately struck by the crispness of the black line art image. If I'd put it into the card as it appeared, it would have seemed jarring or severe. It really needed softening and warming up. The best way to do this was to scan the image and place it in Adobe Photoshop, a wonderful program for enhancing and manipulating images.

I'll just summarize what I did to doctor our Seal. I tried to smooth out the crisp lines and textures, and introduce some continuous tones, by applying a Photoshop filter to the scanned image.

Then I applied some warm colors, such as browns and reds which I brushed onto the eagle. I also accentuated other reds and yellows, and warmed up blues, such as the blue in the round star emblem. Finally, I added the soft tan texture bands behind the eagle. The fully warmed-up seal is shown in Figure 35.

Set 6. Even though the "winner" had been selected, the White House people asked to see some other color combinations—basically, different blues combined with the red bar at the top. I also needed to do more versions for Cromalin proofs, so that I could check colors and make corrections. The hologram idea came back as the wavy flag, then was rejected again, as it was considered not really necessary for anti-counterfeit purposes.

25. A few more final color variations were asked for. What I see on my monitor is not necessarily the colors that will print. We needed to see the final colors in a Cromaline proof.

26,27. The waving flag under the name and Social Security number was to be a hologram, to prevent counterfeiting. It looked too glitzy and busy under the Great Seal. One main symbol (the Seal) and a couple of secondary ones (the stars) is about all a card this size can take without looking crammed.

28. One of the few in which the blue background graduates all the way to the bottom.

29, 30. Still more variations.

31. A solid blue without gradation.

32. The final art.

33. About ten versions were produced of the back of the card. This was the final version.

34. The actual Great Seal image I found revealed a crisp, line-art image. Using it as it was would have put a jarring element into the center of the card. It had to be softened and warmed up.

35. This softening and warming was rendered in Photoshop. I applied a filter to smooth out crisp lines and textures; brushed on browns and reds to thaw out the eagle; accentuated yellows and warmed up blues; and added the soft tan texture bands behind the eagle.

CONCLUSIONS

To create all these many versions of the card design, I didn't have to start from scratch each time. I had basic template elements—image size, type styles, pinstripe styles, star shapes, background colors and fills, emblem elements and positions—in place in FreeHand, so that, whether working at home or on a Macintosh at the Executive Office Building (as I did on several occasions), I could quickly substitute elements or put in new ones.

In this way, subtle or drastic variations could be tried and evaluated very quickly. I now realize more than ever that I made the right decision in 1986 to become a computer-based illustrator, and a home-based one, too.

This was a strenuous, exhausting job. But when my four young excited daughters saw the President hold up their old man's handiwork, I knew it had been worth all the time and effort.

CHAPTER
4.

Managing
Images

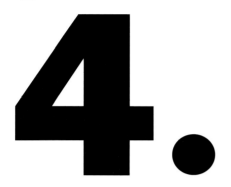

Y ou can make a pretty good analogy between an information illustrator and the curator of a large art museum. If you assume for the sake of pursuing the analogy that both curator and illustrator deal primarily with images, you'll probably agree that they face a set of common problems :

—locating good sources of images, selecting images, and acquiring them
—storing images, and organizing and cataloguing the images so that they can be found when needed
—finding specific images being stored
—retrieving them efficiently

We can refer collectively to these problems, and the daily solutions they demand, as the general area of image management. In this chapter we'll look at a number of specific examples which illustrate good practices in managing your images.

IMAGE SOURCES

Let's say you're already an illustrator. You don't need to be told how to go about getting ideas, images, and information; but let's summarize the main sources anyway, in order to provide some context for the discussion that follows.

If you're like me and most other illustrators I know, you get your ideas primarily from three places: reference pictures from other sources; your own photographs and previous illus-

trations; and your head. The third, of course, often synthesizes a conception from the first two.

We get reference pictures from various places, including picture books, visual encyclopedias, stock photo services, and public archives. Most illustrators are well aware of and experienced with these sources.

To give just one example, I often use the high quality line art illustrations in Dover Publications' *Handbook of Early Advertising Art*. This is one of the largest, if not the largest, compilations of copyright-free early advertising art. It covers the period from the 1780's through the 1890's, and includes both American and European sources. There are over 6,000 high quality line art illustrations, grouped by subject (eg., Agriculture; Animals; Automobiles; Birds; Buildings; Christmas; Clothing; Figures; Flowers). Figure 1 shows some images from the section entitled "Musical Instruments."

You may be aware that reference picture sources are now available in digital form. Commercial clip art files—which no self-respecting illustrator uses, of course—are available both on diskette and on high-capacity, 550-650 megabyte, CD-ROM's (this stands for "Compact Disc, Read-Only Memory").

A more exciting development is that very high quality digitized stock

1. These images from *Handbook of Early Advertising Art* can be used, copyright-free, up to ten at a time.

photograph libraries are now being recorded on CD-ROM's containing an average of 100 photograph-quality images. For a fraction of the cost of buying a stock photo, you can download a photo from the CD and place it directly into your illustration file. Since it is a digital image, it suffers none of the loss of quality that results when you scan in a photo.

ELECTRONIC TRACING

Electronic illustration differs from traditional illustration in the manner in which reference pictures are used as the basis for an image. In the old days, before I switched to the computer, I had to trace over the reference picture (whether a stock photo, archival illustration, or one of my own photographs), and then transfer the tracing to a drawing board.

Things are faster and simpler now. I scan in a reference image, place it in an illustration or paint program, then trace an electronic outline over it. This eliminates a generation—the transfer of the image onto the drawing board. You don't have to redraw your lines a second time, and you get tighter a lot quicker.

For example, I recently did an illustration showing the Heimlich maneuver being applied to a choking person. The first thing to do was have my daughter take a photo of my wife Heimliching the hapless victim, me. I took this photo and scanned it into my system using my black-and-white scanner and scanning software (2).

After putting the scan into Aldus FreeHand (an easy operation), I traced the key outlines of the figures (3, 4), using the Wacom electronic stylus and tablet. When I'd finished the tracing I adjusted the stroke thicknesses and applied colors and shadings (5). The final illustration is shown in Figure 6.

STORING AND CATALOGUING YOUR IMAGES

The images I keep and use in my work are either paper or electronic. I have thousands of illustrations and photographs stored in different disks in my computer system.

And I have four 30-inch-deep file cabinet drawers crammed completely full of clippings from magazines and other publications.

It's ironic, in view of the subject of this book, that I have a much easier time finding an illustration or photograph in the old file cabinet than I do in my hot rod electronic system. There are two reasons for this. First, all the reference clippings are there in one cabinet, not scattered among ten or twelve cabinets. Second, the material is all organized by subject. Even though most of the subjects are fairly general (eg., Cars, Trucks, Sports, Trees, Mountains, Balloons & Blimps, Space), each folder contains all the paper clippings I have on that subject.

By contrast, my electronic images are scattered, in hard disks, CD-ROM's, SyQuests, and magneto-optical disks. True, each of these four sets of disks has its own drive, and (except for the single hard disk) if I'm looking for a specific illustration file, I can plunk one disk after another into a drive and see whether it has the item I'm looking for.

What I and, I'm sure, most of my colleagues have long needed is a way—a software program—to search our entire systems of storage drives with a single find command.

IMAGE MANAGEMENT SOFTWARE

Some sophisticated programs have recently been introduced that let you organize your large and growing illustration archives into visual databases. Although they have different looks and feels, all of them enable you to catalog your image files so that when you're looking for that old fire engine you drew a couple of years ago, you can (1) find the image, (2) preview it without opening its application program, and, if you wish (3) retrieve the image for editing in its application program.

You may be interested in that specific fire engine image. The program will find it for you. But let's say that you'd like to round up *all* the truck images you've got stored in different files on various drives. You can type in a keyword like "Truck," and the programs will bring together small thumbnails of the truck pictures and present them, via a "gallery" image, for you to browse and select from.

Finally, let's get really fancy and say that we want to retrieve *all* the illustrations, photographs, movies, and sounds, related to our subject, that we have tucked away—that's right, most of these programs have multimedia capabilities.

Let's look at the package I'm currently using—Aldus Fetch—and see how it helps me make order out of creative chaos. First, let's look at how you build up your visual database. Then let's use Fetch to find and retrieve some images.

The Fetch User Guide provides a succinct description of the program: "Aldus Fetch is a multi-user, mixed-media database application designed for use in the professional production department. Fetch lets you catalog *items*—images, movies, sounds, and text, for example—in a common visual database, or *catalog*, and then retrieve them from the catalog, regardless of their format, location, or the applications that created them."

In Fetch you start getting control over your large and rapidly growing image archives by cataloguing your files. In cataloguing, you assign *keywords* and (if you choose) short descriptions to "items," the files to be catalogued.

Keywords are words and phrases that identify the key aspects of an item: those features that you'll want to be able to find and retrieve at a later time.

2. My daughter took a photograph of my wife applying the Heimlich maneuver to me. I scanned the photo into my system and opened the scans in FreeHand.

3, 4. I traced the key outlines of the figures with the Wacom electronic stylus and tablet.

The keywords I commonly assign to an image include subjects, client names, unusual techniques, places, proper names, and illustration or image types (eg., pie charts; technical diagrams; maps; photographs).

For example, I recently created an illustration of the Taj Mahal (7). I knew that I might want to find this image in the future, to use in another illustration, or perhaps to put into a sampling of my work that I'm going to send to a prospective client.

So I put it into Fetch. Putting an image file into Fetch is a task comparable in complexity to tying one's shoelaces. Basically, you open a "catalog" (in which you can organize, and search, up to 32,000 images), then drag the (metaphorical) file across the Macintosh's (metaphorical) "desktop" and then (metaphorically) "drop" the file into the Fetch catalog. That's all there is to it.

When you add an item (an image file) to Fetch, the program automatically stores a thumbnail image, plus other information such as filename and file type. But one thing remains

5. After finishing the tracing I applied graphic effects. I put it into the Fetch image cataloguing and retrieval program.

for you to add—the keywords. In order for Fetch to be able to access this file when you do a search, you must assign keywords to it. Figure 8 shows the "Edit Keywords" dialog box for the Taj Mahal image. You simply click on "Add," type in your keywords, then click on "Done" to close the box.

In my case, I usually use a two-level keyword strategy. For most images I try to assign one keyword which identifies the general category an item fits into (in our Taj example, that keyword is "Building"); and several other keywords that identify key aspects of the image that I'll want to be able to search on ("Monument," "India," "Eason & Assoc," and, of course, "Taj Mahal"). After you've added twenty or fifty or a hundred

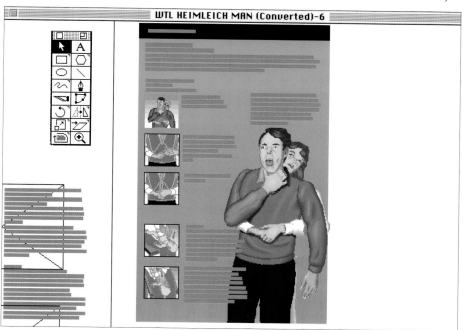

6. The final illustration of the Heimlich maneuver.

items to your visual database (whether using Fetch or one of the other similar programs), you'll begin to see patterns developing in your use of keywords. (You can look at the "master keyword list" on your screen or print it out.)

STRUCTURING YOUR KEYWORD LIST

You'll build a more concise and powerful keyword list if you provide some structure to it at the outset. To catalog my archives, it made most sense to use the set of high-level categories with which I'd already organized my four file drawers full of paper pictures. These categories weren't chosen arbitrarily; they naturally occurred to me because of the nature of my work, which is heavily

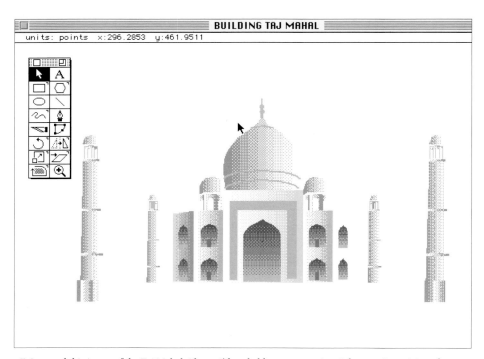

7. I created this image of the Taj Mahal. I knew I'd probably want to retrieve it later, so I put it into the Fetch image cataloguing and retrieval program.

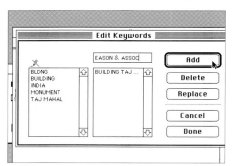

8. Keywords are assigned to the image in this simple dialog box.

FREEHAND N-T 3/

Name	Size	Kind
PEOPL FAM AT SUNST	228K	Aldus FreeHand 3…
PEOPLE -SCIENTIST	78K	Aldus FreeHand 3…
PEOPLE AT COMPUTERS	130K	Aldus FreeHand 3…
PEOPLE AT DOOR	501K	Aldus FreeHand 3…
PEOPLE EYE DOC	72K	Aldus FreeHand 3…
PEOPLE FAM PICNIC	689K	Aldus FreeHand 3…
PEOPLE FAMLIES	332K	Aldus FreeHand 3…
PEOPLE GIRL AT FISH TA…	202K	Aldus FreeHand 3…
PEOPLE IN AIRPLANE	462K	Aldus FreeHand 3…
PEOPLE KID AT COMPUTER	481K	Aldus FreeHand 3…
PEOPLE KIDS AT TABLES	702K	Aldus FreeHand 3…
PEOPLE MAN OUTLINE	52K	Aldus FreeHand 3…
PEOPLE MAN PROFILE	33K	Aldus FreeHand 3…

9. Before programs like Fetch came out, I coordinated my filenames to make them easier to find: for example, these files beginning "People." But this hadn't been done completely or consistently.

oriented toward illustrations concerning structures, machines, technology, and space. Here are some of the categories:

> Aircraft
> Building
> Car

Computer
Machine
People
Space
Technology
Truck

To some extent, I also had used these categories to group together related files on my system: for exam-

ple, seven or eight files beginning "People" (9). But I hadn't been consistent in doing it. However, when I started cataloguing files in Fetch, I could attach "People," or one of its subcategories like "Man" or "Child," as keywords to *all* the files I wanted to be able to retrieve whenever I wanted people images.

If you construct a similar set of high-level categories that reflects the emphases in your body of work, you'll be able to do a search that nets you everything you have in your files on a general subject. Alternatively, the more specific keywords you assign for subcategories or proper names (eg., "Taj Mahal" or "Dump truck" or "Hummingbird" or "Whittle Communications") will enable you to retrieve everything you have on one of these things or names.

If you want to take the time, or can hire a database indexing consultant, you can construct an elegant and powerful hierarchical system that relates general categories and more specific subcategories in the same way that library classifications do. For example, you can organize your keywords for buildings and structures like this:

> Building
> (use for Structures)
>> Barn
>> Church
>> Factory
>> Government building
>> Nuclear power plant
>> Office building

Oil rig
Radio tower
Skyscraper

A system like this—a controlled keyword system—will result in more consistent cataloguing and more accurate and complete searches. By looking at your classification system (on screen or on paper) you'll see, for example, that if you want to find all the images you have on structures in general, the phrase "use for Structures" tells you that you'll find them catalogued under the keyword "Building." Or assume that you're ready to catalog an image of a derrick. Scanning the list tells you that this image should get the keyword "Oil rig" and not "Derrick"—so that later on you'll find it when you do a search on "Oil rig." Without such a controlled list you tend to use various synonymous keywords for the same thing, which completely defeats your purpose.

I haven't yet had the time to organize my keywords into a system like this. I plan to hire a professional database indexer to do the job, someone who specializes in "file crunching" and could save me many hours of boring work that I have trouble devoting precious time to.

FETCHING IMAGES

Now let's look at Fetch in action, finding and retrieving image files. I've been hired to do a complex illustration showing the basic operation of a new wireless communication system, and one thing I need are several different buildings to put into

the scene. Where do I find them? I want to assemble my building images and browse through them.

First I open the "Find window" in Fetch, and type in the keyword "Building" (10). Fetch now goes to work and searches for all of my files to which I've assigned this keyword.

(You can, alternatively, use an expanded Find window which allows you to do more complex searches by combining keywords, file names, and other tags. See Figure 11).

It's important to remember that

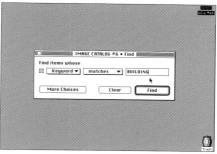

10. I want to find all the image files I have containing buildings, so I execute a search in Fetch on the keyword "Building."

12. The gallery window presents an assembly of thumbnail pictures—the results of the search on the keyword "Building."

Fetch searches for files that are stored not only on the drive you're currently in and not only on the disk currently mounted in that drive—it searches all disks in all drives. (It can do this because it has already stored the information—the thumbnail of the image, the file information, the keywords, and any description you've attached—at the time you put it into Fetch and catalogued it.) For me this is a tremendous timesaving advantage—no longer do I have to put in, search through, and take out disk after disk in a frustrating effort

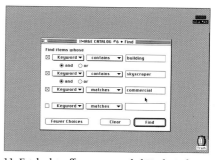

11. Fetch also offers an expanded Find window for complex searches. For example, this box is asking Fetch to find every image that contains "Skyscraper" and "Commercial" as keywords.

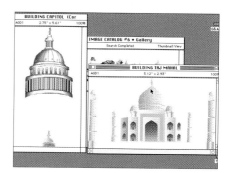

13. I want to see two of the thumbnails, the Taj Mahal and the U.S. Capitol, in full size, so I have Fetch bring up a Preview of them—without opening the application program and file containing the images.

to find something!

Fetch presents the search results, the assembled thumbnail images, in a Gallery window (12). I can scroll up and down through the gallery, browsing at the thumbnails, and if one catches my eye, I can select it and "preview" it.

Two of the images have indeed caught my eye, the Taj Mahal and the U.S. Capitol, so I execute the preview command and Fetch displays full-size replicas of the images in the Preview window (13). It does this without opening the image file in its application—another timesaving feature.

You can preview multiple images at the same time to compare them; and you can set aside the items you're interested in (in a "pasteboard") as you do other searches.

If, instead of visually browsing the gallery, I want information on the files which the search has netted, I bring up the Text List window, which lists the file name, file type, and system location for all the items (14).

If I want to see any images, I simply highlight the file name and Fetch displays the thumbnail, keywords, and associated description in a Text List Window (14).

Finally, after having previewed the Taj Mahal and U.S. Capitol images, and having decided that I do want to use it in the new illustration, I choose the "Edit Original" command. This tells Fetch to open the image file's source application, which in turn

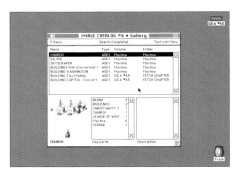

14. If you bring up the Text List window, you get a listing of filenames, file types, and system location for each item that a search has uncovered.

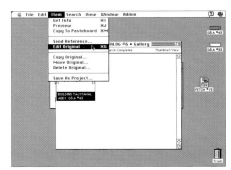

15. With a simple command, Fetch opens the Taj file's source application (FreeHand), which in turns opens the file for editing.

16. The edited Taj Mahal image, along with the U.S. Capitol image, is finally used in the new illustration.

opens (for example) the Taj Mahal file for editing (15). After editing I take it and use it in the new illustration (16), along with the image of the U.S. Capitol (12)..

INDEX